40p

Lynne

by

Mirabelle Maslin

Augur Press

LYNNE
Copyright © Mirabelle Maslin 2011

The moral right of the author has been asserted

Author of:
Beyond the Veil
Tracy
Carl and other writings
Fay
On a Dog Lead
Emily
The Fifth Key
The Candle Flame
The Supply Teacher's Surprise
Miranda

British Library Cataloguing in Publication Data.
A catalogue record for this book is available from the British Library.

ISBN 978-0-9558936-6-7

First published 2011 by
Augur Press
Delf House,
52, Penicuik Road,
Roslin,
Midlothian EH25 9LH
United Kingdom

Printed and bound in Great Britain by CPI Antony Rowe,
Chippenham and Eastbourne

Lynne

To all readers who enjoy my writing

Chapter One

Lynne left the office seething with rage. Oh yes, she knew this kind of thing was all too common nowadays, but she had never thought it would happen to her. Her cousin Maddie had had a very bad time at work the previous year, and Lynne had done her best to support her through it. The problem there had been so obvious. New, but inexperienced, managerial staff had been brought in, and the workforce had suffered as a result. This had never been acknowledged, and instead staff had been blamed for low productivity.

She thought about how outraged she had felt on Maddie's behalf. Maddie was very experienced at her work with pension plans at a large insurance company. Low productivity could never have been an issue where her output was concerned, yet along with the others, she had been falsely blamed. The rub was that Maddie herself should have been part of the management team, and the only reason why she hadn't looked for promotion was to do with the fact that she took her commitments to her family very seriously, and did not want to take on more responsibility for a few more years.

Lynne tried to walk at a leisurely pace across the car park. Her whole body was telling her to stamp every step, and to storm her way between the tightly packed vehicles, but caution led her to hide this impulse and appear normal.

'Normal!' she sneered angrily, although her voice was barely audible. 'I don't think I know any more what normal is.'

Her neat flat shoes made no sound as she made her way smoothly towards her car. Any observer would have seen only a smartly dressed woman in her mid-thirties, her light brown hair in well-contained waves, and it would have been easy to assume that she was employed at a managerial level.

It had been just after lunchtime that day when she received the e-mail from Lucy, her new manager. Everything had seemed fine until then. But now her world had been turned upside down, and by someone who was nearly ten years younger than herself.

Lucy had been transferred from another department. Lynne's first sight of her had left her thinking that she must be a particularly well-dressed school leaver. Later, she was surprised to learn that this was her new manager, and that she was twenty-seven. She had been presented as a kind of whizz-kid who was going to revamp things, sweeping away old cobwebs and modernising the department. But in reality she was stupid. Yes, stupid. She had all the jargon and buzzwords on the tip of her tongue, but she knew nothing about people and real management.

For the hundredth time in the space of the last hour, Lynne wished that Sarah, her previous manager, had never been promoted. She had felt so happy for her when the news first came through. Sarah had been the manager since long before she herself had joined the department, four years ago. Sarah had been just fifty when the promotion came through. She certainly deserved it. All that hard work and dedication she had put in had brought its reward. What Lynne herself had valued most was her kindly yet firm and realistic approach. Within only a few days of starting work, she had become confident about working under her. She had soon come to realise that Sarah was a very intelligent woman, who always worked towards the best outcome for everyone. Employer and employee alike benefited from her presence. The department had been a happy place, with little sickness and no absenteeism.

She reached the relative safety of her car, hurriedly unlocked the door and sat in the driving seat. Here she felt in some kind of control. Her mind revisited Lucy's e-mail and the meeting afterwards. The message had said that there was a problem with the standard of her work, and that she was to see Lucy in interview room two, at three o'clock that day. She had mistakenly thought that whatever the problem was, it could easily be ironed out, and she had entered the room confidently, ready to identify the source of the misunderstanding.

However, she had soon discovered that the scenario was quite different from what she had imagined. When Lynne entered the room, she found that there was a stranger with Lucy, and that they were both seated behind a desk. The stranger was introduced as Pattie from HR. Lynne judged that she must be in her late fifties. She was one of those people who looked as if she not only wore a suit to work, but also went to bed in one. She was gaunt, with a tight expression on her face, and her hair was scraped back into what Lynne imagined must be a small bun. She took an instant dislike to her.

Lucy indicated that she should sit down. She complied, and soon it became apparent that her instinct about Pattie had been well-founded. Pattie opened a bulky file that had lain closed on the desk in front of her, selected some documents, and passed them to Lucy. With distaste Lynne noticed a smirk on Lucy's face.

She waited, and Pattie began.

'Inadequate performance and unacceptable behaviour,' she stated.

Lynne could not conceal her reaction. 'That's ridiculous!' she exclaimed. All her plans of examining a misunderstanding had disappeared.

Then Lucy spoke. 'We have records here.'

'Yes,' Pattie confirmed, 'a complaint has been made against you.'

'But... but I've been here for four years, and have an unblemished record,' Lynne protested.

'We are aware of that,' said Pattie smoothly. 'Obviously you've been slipping.'

'There must be some mistake,' said Lynne in a strangled voice that she barely recognised. She became aware that Pattie was scribbling something down on a fresh sheet of paper. 'What's that?' she questioned.

'I'm taking notes of the meeting,' Pattie replied tersely. 'This is a serious matter.'

'Is there something wrong at home?' asked Lucy sweetly.

Lynne nearly fell for this, but managed to stop herself just in time. They already knew that she had taken her mother to hospital a fortnight ago, because of the day she took off at short notice. Secretly, she dug her fingernails into the palms of her hands. What they did not know was that her mother's health was still not good, and that her own beloved dog, Bracken, had died only last week, and she was bereft without him. She definitely wasn't going to give them that information.

'You were about to say something,' Lucy prompted.

'No,' said Lynne. 'I just thought I needed to clear my throat.' She slid her right hand under her left, and crossed two of its fingers. 'Everything's fine at home.'

'So, have you any explanation as to why you've been slipping so badly?' Lucy probed.

'I haven't,' said Lynne.

'No explanation?' Pattie's voice was grim. 'You must have some idea.' She continued to scribble furiously.

'I meant that I haven't been slipping.'

'Now you're contradicting yourself,' said Lucy gleefully.

Pattie turned to Lucy and said in clipped tones, 'I think this is sufficient for the preliminary meeting.' She shut the file briskly and stood up.

Lynne was alarmed. 'But we haven't sorted anything out yet.'

'That's because you're refusing to cooperate,' snapped Pattie. 'Inadequate performance, inappropriate behaviour and refusal to cooperate. Extremely serious. You'll receive a written report within the week.'

Lucy consulted her watch and announced, 'I should be in another meeting now.'

She picked up the documents that lay in front of her, and strutted out of the room with Pattie close behind her, leaving Lynne staring after them.

4

Lynne returned to her desk, tears welling up in her eyes. She could not see her computer screen through the veil of tears, and went to the toilets to lock herself in a cubicle for privacy.

When at last she thought she might try to work again, there was only half an hour of the day left, so she decided to leave earlier than usual. She normally worked until five, but the flexi-time arrangements meant that she could leave now, and catch up later.

Having thought this far, she turned the key in the ignition of her car, and was soon driving homewards.

When she opened the front door of her compact semi-detached bungalow, its terrible emptiness hit her yet again. Bracken had been a good friend and companion for fifteen years, who by his very presence and loyalty had supported her through a number of crises. Bracken had been a gift from her father, not long before his untimely death.

She switched the radio on to try to fill the void, but somehow its only effect was to enhance the emptiness, and she silenced it. When Bracken had been alive, a feeling of cosy warmth had been engendered by the presence of his warm body and his responsiveness towards her, together with the sound of the radio voices in the background. However, today the radio was not only an irritation, but also aggravated her anger and distress.

Half-heartedly, she tried phoning the home number of one of her work colleagues, but there was no reply, and she left no message. She wished fervently that she could speak to Sarah, but she knew that she was on leave at the moment, visiting her family. Why, oh why should she be away at a time like this? Her advice would be invaluable.

She knew that she should phone her mother to see how she was, but she was afraid she would sense that there was something wrong. She didn't want to worry her. After all, her mother needed all her strength to prepare for her next hospitalisation, which would involve surgery.

She wrestled with herself, uncertain about what to do. In

the end she sent a text to say that she'd had a long day, was going to bed early, and would ring for a chat the following day. A reply came back almost straight away, wishing her a good night's sleep. This was her mother through and through – forever understanding of the needs of others. Lynne hated having to employ deception, but she reassured herself that it was for a good reason.

Lynne ate only a little, and went to bed early. The next morning she woke with a terrible migraine headache, and phoned in sick. She was very unwell, and stayed in bed for much of the day. By the time the evening came, she was completely exhausted. She phoned her mother around eight, and when she explained that she'd had a migraine, her mother was predictably sympathetic. There was no need to attempt to disguise her vulnerable state, since her mother understandably put it down to the aftermath of the migraine. Before she rang off, she promised that she would go round on Saturday as usual, to spend the day together and to pick up any shopping that her mother needed.

Chapter Two

The next day was Friday. The headache had cleared, although she felt washed out. Lynne rose early so that she could get ready slowly.

She heard the familiar rattle of the letterbox as the postman delivered some mail, and she went to collect it from the mat where it had fallen. Phone bill, advertising literature... But what was this? She examined the bulky A5 size white envelope that she now held in her hand. Her name and address were on the front in handwriting that looked vaguely familiar. She felt a sense of unease as she opened it by slicing a thin sliver off the end with the kitchen scissors.

She stared at the contents in disbelief. She now knew that the round, clear, slightly juvenile, handwriting that appeared on the envelope was Lucy's. There was a warning letter, a copy of the minutes of that stupid meeting she'd had to attend, and several sheets stapled together that were headed 'complaints procedure'.

Her eyes skimmed the letter. 'Inadequate performance, inappropriate behaviour, and refusal to cooperate.' The words seem to leap at her accusingly from the page. Her eyes filled with tears. It was so unfair! And what was this? From now on her work was to be closely supervised... by her junior. This was crazy! She read through the minutes.

'But I didn't say that!' she shouted loudly. 'I didn't!' She read on, and found to her horror that everything she had said was misrepresented. 'I'll get this sorted out once and for all,' she proclaimed angrily.

But then she froze. There had only been three people at that meeting. There had been no independent witness to what she had really said, and the other two were bound to close ranks. It was a set-up! But why? 'Why me?' she said through angrily gritted teeth. After all, she was an asset to the team. Admittedly she had not worked there as long as some, but she was certainly very proficient.

Then it began to dawn on her what the problem might be. This was Lucy's first managerial post, and she probably felt threatened. How sick can you get? But how had she managed to enlist the aid of Pattie? That was certainly a puzzle, and one that she needed to get to the bottom of, if she were to remain working there.

She glanced at her watch. Good, there was still plenty of time before she had to leave, and she started to read through the complaints procedure. 'Stage one: identification of complaint and verbal warning.' What verbal warning? There had been none. Well, she'd got them there.

But had she? The way things were shaping up, she could guess that Lucy was completely capable of fabricating a statement that she had issued a verbal warning. 'And if I say she's lying, I expect that'll be added to the list of my fictitious inappropriate behaviour,' Lynne muttered mutinously.

She slumped heavily on to one of the kitchen chairs, and put her head in her hands. This wasn't exactly the same as Maddie had gone through at the beginning, but it was looking worryingly similar.

After a few minutes, she rallied, and read on to discover that if there were continuing problems, the next stage would be a disciplinary hearing. 'About what?' she sneered. 'I haven't done anything wrong yet. How can I "improve" and avoid a "hearing"?' Once again, she sagged. She felt defeated. Bracken was gone, Mum was still ill and heading for surgery, through no fault of her own her job was at risk, and she seemed fated not to find a partner for herself. Her mind began to fill with her last abortive attempt to find a man to share her life, but very determinedly she shut off the memories. 'No good going over that again,' she said aloud.

She collected her belongings and drove to work.

That day was truly awful.   Her junior kept nosing unhelpfully into her work in an ill-informed way, and Lucy strutted round the office with a smirk on her face.   Lynne was completely exhausted when she left at the end of the afternoon, and she knew without any doubt that she was going to have to do something to change her life.

That weekend, she valued every minute of the day she spent with her mother, Audrey.   It was one of Audrey's better days. Her face had a little colour in it, so that her loss of weight and her grey thinning hair seemed less pronounced.   In the morning she managed to go with Lynne to the shops, and although she had to sit down for much of the time, they both enjoyed the outing.   After her mother's lunchtime rest, they sat and talked.

'I'm going to have to change jobs, Mum,' Lynne began.

'I had a feeling there was something wrong.   What's happened?'

'Remember how Maddie was bullied and victimised?'

'Yes, how could I forget? It was awful.'

'Well, something similar has started up for me.'

'That's terrible. Is there anything I can do?'

Lynne smiled. 'Yes, you can get well.'

'That's not what I mean.'

'But it's what *I* mean, and I think we're going to have to put our minds to what we can do.   We've been relying on the hospital so far, but I think we need to look beyond it as well.'

'I'll have to have my operation.'

'I know, but after that.'

'They've said I should be fine, and I'll have checkups.'

'Yes, that's what they usually do with this kind of problem.'

'To be honest, I'd assumed that because your gran died of severe bowel problems, I was likely to go the same way.'

Lynne had never known her mother's mother, as she had died before she was born. 'Remember that sixty is still young these days,' Lynne stated determinedly.   'I think we should consider using some of Dad's money to get good advice about how to make sure you get properly well from this. It's a warning – that's all.'

Lynne had not spoken to her mother before in such a forthright way about her illness. They had a close relationship, but it had never involved her mother confiding more deeply about her illness. Lynne had assumed that this had been her choice, and had respected it by taking only a supportive role. But now she felt differently, and was ready to challenge any beliefs that her mother had that seemed dated. She was surprised to notice that this change seemed to result in her feeling less beset by her work situation, but bearing in mind that this was Saturday, she delayed her final judgement on this.

'Mum,' she said suddenly, 'I'm going to apply for some unpaid leave for when you come home from hospital. A month at least.'

'But what about your career?' said Audrey anxiously. 'Won't it count against you?'

'I don't think it'll make a jot of difference,' Lynne replied. 'There's already something going on against me. I can't pretend to understand what it's really about, and the way things are shaping up they may well get rid of me anyway. The best thing is to lead my life in the way I think is right. I haven't got any dependants, and that leaves me free to make my own decisions.'

'It would be so lovely to have you with me. The neighbours have been clubbing together to fix something up, but I was feeling worried about it all.'

'Well, just tell them that your daughter will be coming to stay for a few weeks, and that they'll be very welcome to call in, and if they can help you with shopping and company after that, we'll be very grateful.'

Lynne watched her mother's face as it relaxed. The years seemed to fall away from her. The lines of worry and stress faded, and she looked more herself than she had since Dad had died.

Lynne went on. 'Mum, we've got a long future together. I can feel it.' She paused for a few minutes before continuing.

'I've thought a bit about practical things. You've got Dad's money, and I've got quite a lot of equity in my house, so it'll be easy to borrow some money on that to tide me over. And don't say that I can have some of Dad's money. It's yours,' she finished firmly.

'I think I'd better have another lie down,' said Audrey. 'I've got a lot to think about.'

Lynne busied herself until suppertime by doing some cleaning and clearing out. She didn't throw anything away. Instead, she laid out everything she thought could be discarded, ready for her mother's agreement. She took food to her on a tray, and sat with her while she ate.

'I've got some more ideas,' she stated.

'Tell me about them.'

Lynne noted with satisfaction that her mother was not only eating the food, but she was actually enjoying it.

'Next weekend I want us to do some research,' Lynne announced.

'What have you got in mind?'

'With Bracken gone, I think we could offer a home to an ageing pet. What do you think?'

'That's a lovely idea, dear!' Audrey exclaimed with an enthusiasm that had grown all too rare over the last months. Then she looked uncertain and added, 'But do you think we'll be able to manage?'

'We'll have to choose carefully,' said Lynne. 'I once knew someone who took on a dog that had belonged to an elderly man who'd had to go into a care home.' She laughed. 'The dog behaved like a gentleman. You should have seen how he got on and off buses – a perfect passenger.'

'I think we could give a home to a dog like that,' Audrey agreed, regaining her confidence. 'Even in my state of health, I could let a dog in and out of the back garden, and if you could leave me enough food for it, I'm sure I could manage. Yes, let's do some research next weekend.'

'Good, that's decided.'

'And now I've got something I want to talk to *you* about,' said her mother, suddenly changing tack.

'Go on,' Lynne replied, intrigued.

'I don't want to look as if I'm meddling in your affairs, but sometimes I worry about where you're going in your life since you and Larry...'

'Mum, I don't want you to mention that name ever again,' Lynne stated firmly. 'I've put all that behind me.'

Lynne's mother looked as if she were going to say something else, but then seemed to change her mind. Lynne stood up and stared fixedly out of the window for a few minutes, saying nothing.

When she returned to the chair beside her mother's bed, she said, 'I'm sorry. I shouldn't have been sharp with you. Were you going to say something else about that whole sorry mess?'

'I'd like to have a long talk with you about it, but I don't want to force anything on you,' her mother replied tentatively.

'I might find that hard, but I think you're probably right that this is the time for it,' Lynne conceded. 'However, I'd prefer it if we don't mention his name. Why don't you lie down again, and I'll lie on the other side of the bed?'

'That's a good idea,' her mother agreed.

Lynne took the tray, put it outside on the landing, and lay on the bed with her mother. 'Now, where shall we start?' she asked. But without waiting for a response to her question, she began. 'There might be things I'll say that you haven't known before. For instance, you probably don't know that he'd been married before we met.'

'I certainly hadn't known that. Go on.'

'He was newly divorced when I first met him at the badminton club, but of course I didn't know that then.'

'You met him the day before your thirtieth birthday,' her mother commented.

'You remembered!'

'I don't usually forget things like that. You were glowing when you came round to see me on your birthday, and I guessed there must be someone on the horizon.'

A shadow of pain passed across Lynne's face as she said, almost whispering, 'He so reminded me of Dad at first.'

'Me, too. He seemed so gentle and considerate to begin with.'

' "To begin with" sums it up,' said Lynne wryly. 'But the beginning went on for a good two years, and by that time I had no doubts that it was all real and forever.'

'I remember the day you got engaged. You looked so happy, and I wished your father had been there to see you.'

'I'm glad he never knew him,' said Lynne emphatically.

'Everything seemed to be progressing. You bought that nice ground-floor flat together, and the wedding day was fixed. I remember liking the fact that neither of you was wanting to rush things, and there was plenty of time to prepare – nearly a whole year. Lynne, when did you start to suspect that something was wrong?'

'When I look back, there had been signs from just after we got engaged. Why I ignored them, I don't know.'

'Once you think you feel sure of a person, it's all too easy to avoid facing the truth, especially if it's hard,' said her mother compassionately.

Lynne felt tears welling up in her eyes. 'I didn't want to lose him,' she choked out. 'It felt as if I would lose Dad all over again.'

'I had a bit of that myself,' her mother confessed. 'I saw that something wasn't quite right, and I turned a blind eye to it instead of asking you about it. Looking back, I can see I didn't want to lose him either. I feel guilty about that now, as if I let you down.'

'Oh, Mum!' Lynne exclaimed. 'You shouldn't have felt like that. I was a grown woman by then.'

'Once a mother, always a mother.' Audrey took her daughter's hand. 'Lynne, do you want to have a child yourself?' she asked gently.

Lynne began to draw her hand away, and then stopped,

realising what she was doing. 'Well, actually... yes,' she confided.

'You mustn't leave it much longer,' her mother advised.

'I know that, but there's no one in sight, and I can't have a baby without there being a father.'

'I mean don't leave it much longer before you try to trust a man again.'

'It's very difficult. If I feel drawn to someone, I just remember the badminton club, and then I walk off in the opposite direction. Mum, I had a very lucky escape.'

'Yes, you did. A violent ex-convict.'

'He'd well-nigh crippled his wife,' said Lynne quietly.

'Lynne, I wish you'd been able to tell me that before.'

'I wanted to, but at the same time I didn't want you to know the size of the mistake I'd made. Even when he knew I'd found out about everything, he tried to smooth things over. He lied about how serious it was, but by that time I knew it all, and I wasn't taken in. I'd collected all the proof I needed, and when I confronted him I made sure that there were plenty of people around.'

'That party was ingenious.'

'It was more like desperation. I knew I had to end my contact with him, but by that time I was very afraid of him. I thought if I arranged the kind of party that he liked he wouldn't suspect anything. I invited everyone I could think of, and I wrote out what I was going to say.'

'How you managed to go through more than two hours of the party before you did it, I'll never know.'

'Neither will I! I was shaking like a leaf underneath that beautiful new dress I'd bought specially for the occasion. I stood in the centre of the room and called for silence. Probably everyone thought I was going to toast our future. They picked up their glasses and waited. I could never have gone through with it if I hadn't had it all written down in advance. After I'd finished, I made myself look at him. He looked completely calm, and at first protested his innocence, and then tried to minimise what he'd done. Then I got out the photocopies of newspaper reports that I'd secretly collected as proof. It was then that he changed. He looked as if he was going to explode. I asked everyone to stay while he collected his things. Several people stayed the night with me, and I had the locks changed the next day.'

'I was so proud of you when I heard what you'd done.'

'Mum, how am I ever going to trust anyone again?'

'Well, you're not going to if you keep avoiding trying.'

'It's been nearly three years,' said Lynne, half to herself, 'and next birthday I'll be thirty-six.'

'That's not too late.'

'Nearly.'

'Not too late,' her mother repeated firmly.

'Bracken was with me through it all, but now he's gone too,' said Lynne sadly. 'I'm glad I got a buyer for the flat so quickly. The solicitor dealt with the splitting of the money, and you and I found my present home without any difficulty. Mum, would you like to live in a house like mine?' she asked suddenly.

'Why do you ask?'

'There are sometimes ones quite nearby that come on to the market, and I was thinking how nice it would be if we lived closer to each other. As you know, most of the accommodation is on one level, and that might suit you better as time goes on.'

'You could be right. I haven't wanted to think about leaving this house that I shared with your dad for so many years, but I do sometimes worry about the bathroom and all the bedrooms being upstairs. I won't be able to do anything until I'm well, but can you keep me up to date about local properties that come on to the market?'

Lynne noticed this was the first time that her mother had spoken about getting well, and she felt very pleased. 'Of course, I will,' she assured her. 'And now I think you should get ready for the night. I'll tuck you in, but then I'll have to go home. There are things I have to see to, but I'll give you a ring tomorrow as usual.'

'You mustn't hide anything from me about the work situation,' her mother said worriedly. 'If I thought you were, it would be more stressful than knowing the real position, however bad it might be.'

Lynne thought for a moment. 'I don't like the idea of burdening you with it, but I can see what you mean. Okay, I'll keep you up to date.'

Chapter Three

Lynne spent Sunday evening quietly preparing herself for the following day at the office. She felt sure that things would not have eased, and quite probably would be worse. But even so she was not prepared for what took place.

The first thing she noticed was that no one acknowledged her presence when she arrived. It was as if she didn't exist. The second thing was a sinister white envelope on her desk. And the third thing was the size of Lucy's smirk.

Slowly she opened the envelope. The letter inside informed her that absenteeism had been added to the list of her crimes.

She didn't start work. Instead, she wrote an e-mail request for five weeks of unpaid leave, to start one week after her mother's operation. She sent it off, although in her heart she knew that in any case she couldn't face working in this atmosphere for much longer.

Only then did she turn to the week's allocation of files that had been balanced on the edge of her desk. She thumbed through the first three, to find that she had been given very difficult time-consuming tasks. She was about to start work, when she decided to check the other files. Her suspicions were confirmed. These files contained knotty problems, each of which would require at least a day's work. And now she knew that she was being set up to fail, as there was no way that she could work her way through this allocation by the end of Friday.

She worked skilfully and methodically through the problems that the first file presented, but it took nearly the whole day. At four o'clock she began work on the next file. Mentally she had decided to stay late, but at one minute to five, Lucy came to speak to her.

'You can't stay after five,' she informed her, with her

increased smirk now seeming to cover the whole of her face. One hand was hidden behind her back.

'I'm sure the rules say six,' Lynne replied, refusing to rise to the bait.

'They've changed,' said Lucy. She whipped her hidden hand into view and revealed yet another letter.

Lynne studied it. It seemed that there were now four complaints against her: she was not allowed to be in the office without supervision from Lucy, and it was clear that Lucy was about to leave. Silently, she closed down her computer and reassembled the contents of the file she had been working on. She picked up her bag from beside her desk and went to retrieve her coat from her locker, where she found that the lock had been jammed, and she couldn't open it. An image came into her mind, unbidden, of winding the long strap of her handbag round Lucy's neck and tightening it. She pushed it out of her thoughts and walked out of the office with as sedate a pace as she could muster. She headed for her car, deliberately ignoring the fact that Lucy was lurking beside the exit door, exuding the smell of expensive perfume.

She drove to a nearby side street, where she parked, waiting for her knees to stop vibrating. Her feelings were a mixture of rage and distress. The former led her to feel murderous, and the latter left her wanting to collapse. It took a full half hour for the worst to pass, and it was a further fifteen minutes before she felt safe to drive.

At home, she phoned Sarah, knowing that she would be back from holiday. She hadn't meant to phone her so soon, but couldn't wait. She had to tell someone about what Lucy was doing, even if there was no way of stopping her. When she heard the familiar sound of Sarah's calm measured tones, she realised how hard it had been waiting to speak to her.

'Hello, Sarah here.'

'It's Lynne. How was your holiday?'

'Oh, Lynne. It's lovely to hear from you. I've had a wonderful holiday, thanks. How's your mum?'

'It won't be long now before she has her op. Just another two weeks or so. I've applied for five weeks unpaid leave for when she comes back home, but I've a hunch that I won't be at work for much longer.'

'What do you mean?'

'I don't want to load you with my problems, but I'd appreciate your thoughts on what's happening.'

'What's that?'

'Your replacement is no replacement at all, and she's targeted me,' said Lynne cryptically.

'To be honest, when I heard who they were going to put in my place, I felt very uneasy. What's she up to?'

'Everything I do or say is being changed into something else, and as a result there's a growing list of complaints against me.'

'That's awful, and it's so unfounded. You are the kind of employee that every employer values.'

'Well, the truth of the matter is that the manager is doing everything she can to cast me in the worst light possible, and I wouldn't put it past her to engineer my removal from the team.'

Sarah groaned. 'I've heard so much about this kind of thing, although this is the first time within our organisation. Have you been given a copy of the complaints procedure?'

'Yes, and I can see that it isn't being followed properly at all. Actually, I've been wondering about seeing a solicitor who knows about employment law.'

'I don't know how far you'll get,' said Sarah worriedly. 'I don't like to sound pessimistic, but if you don't find someone who really knows their job, you can end up in an even worse position. Have you thought of going to the union?'

'Yes, but as you know, here it's just another part of the organisation. It isn't independent.'

'I want to help, but I can't think how.'

'Look, Sarah,' said Lynne, 'it isn't your battle to fight. It's an enormous help to have a friend like you that I can talk to about it. Mum's made me promise to tell her how things are going, but I don't want to stress her with all the details.'

'You're right. She's vulnerable at the moment, and will be for quite some time. Lynne, you do know that you can phone me any time, don't you?'

'I wasn't sure about that. After all, it's a work thing. Thanks a lot.'

Lynne sighed as she put down the phone. There had been no question about how off-beam Lucy's behaviour was, yet the effect of it had somehow made her begin to question her reality. Now that she had spoken to Sarah, she felt back on track. Her years under Sarah had been entirely trouble-free, and working for the team had been a pleasure and an inspiration. She remembered how each day would start with a feeling of enthusiasm, which would persist despite any difficulties that had to be surmounted. In a few short weeks Lucy's presence had destroyed all that, and had put in its place a feeling of uncertainty and dread. Fleetingly she wondered how the others in the team were feeling, but she knew that there was no point in trying to speak to them. They were clearly under orders not to communicate with her, and for most of them, fear of losing their employment was a central consideration.

She made a decision to take each day as it came, and try hard not to rise to any bait that Lucy laid for her. It was a hard challenge, but she would do her best. Realistically it would be better to keep this job, at least until her mother was well again, so that would be her objective. And meantime, there were things to look forward to. There was the start of their search for a suitable dog, and there was her need to think again about whether or not she would look for a partner for herself, and have the chance of creating her own family.

The week was hard – very hard. As she had expected, Lucy did everything she could to make her life as uncomfortable as possible. Lynne remained flawlessly polite, and continued to work to her usual high standard, all the while keeping her eyes open for trouble. At times she felt as if she had grown sensors all round her head.

Lucy had even stooped to the ploy of spilling a hot drink all over her desk. She had come over on the pretext of checking on Lynne's work, placed her waxed cardboard container of milky coffee right in the middle of the desk, and then deliberately knocked it over while staring insolently into Lynne's eyes. 'Oh, what a shame, you've lost the rest of your drink,' Lynne had made herself say in light tones. 'I'll just get a cloth.' The damage had not been too bad. When she had noticed Lucy advancing with a glint in her eyes, Lynne had taken the precaution of heaping everything on her desk in one pile and putting it on one side, as if clearing it to begin another task. Thus she was ready for the spill in case it came. Lucy had planted her drink, waited, and then as she reached forward to spill it, Lynne whipped the heap of documents off the desk, and the milky mess failed to reach them. Even then she had taken the precaution of carrying the documents with her as she went to fetch the cloth, and when she returned, Lucy had gone.

There was no response yet to her request for unpaid leave, but it was still a little soon for a decision to have been made. Lynne felt uncomfortable about the fact that Lucy would thus find out that her mother was still ill, but she'd just have to face that when it happened. This would be the hardest thing to deal with because it was the most personal, and was likely to be the most hurtful.

Chapter Four

Saturday came, and Lynne bought a local newspaper, which she took with her to her mother's house.

'Let's look in this for clues,' she suggested as she sat down. She found the pet column. 'Not a lot here. Hamsters, rabbits, budgies…'

Audrey made no comment, but was aware of feeling disappointed.

'Wait a minute, this might lead to something,' Lynne announced. 'Good home wanted for elderly collie.'

Audrey leaned forward. 'What else does it say?'

'It just gives a mobile number.'

'Let's try it.' Audrey picked up the phone and Lynne read out the number. There was no reply, so she left a message. 'What else shall we do?'

'Yellow pages?' asked Lynne. She collected the directory from the bookshelves, and handed it to her mother. They studied it together, but found nothing that helped them.

'We could try the local cat and dog home,' said Audrey uncertainly, 'but I'm not terribly keen.'

'How about going round to have a look?'

'All right. We might learn something.'

Lynne found the address, and soon they were on their way.

When they arrived, there was no one to be seen. There was a gate in the wire mesh fence that surrounded it, but it was locked. A notice advised them to press a buzzer. Loud barking began immediately. They waited, and eventually a cheerful energetic red-haired girl let them in.

'I work here doing relief at weekends,' she explained.

'We've come to find out about adopting a dog,' Lynne told her.

'I'm on my own here today,' said the girl, 'and all I can do is show you round. If you're interested in any of the dogs, you'll have to come back on Monday to speak to the manager.'

Lynne and her mother could see how the animals rushed forward in their compounds to nuzzle the girl affectionately as she passed by.

'We're looking for a quiet animal,' said Lynne.

'Yes,' her mother confirmed. 'Preferably we want one that's belonged to an older person.'

'We might not be able to take a dog until my mother's home from hospital,' Lynne explained.

'Don't worry about that. If you find one that you want, we can look after it here for a few weeks. We can put your name on it once your home has been assessed.'

Although Lynne and her mother enjoyed seeing the dogs, neither of them felt particularly drawn to any one of them. They thanked the girl, and went home to discover that there was a phone message from the owner of the collie.

'I'll have to lie down for an hour before I can do anything else,' Audrey decided.

'I could ring and let the person know that we'd be available tomorrow,' Lynne offered. 'I can tell you about the call when you come back downstairs.'

Making an arrangement to see the collie turned out to be straightforward. Lynne took a note of the address and agreed to arrive around noon the following day.

On Sunday they arrived in good time in a street of well-kept bungalows. Lynne parked the car, and they waited for a few minutes.

'The gardens look nice,' Audrey remarked.

'Yes, I like the feel of this street,' Lynne replied. 'Let's go and ring the bell now.'

The door was answered promptly by a plump woman with friendly manner, who Lynne guessed must be in her fifties.

'I'm Pauline Pritchard. Come on in. We'll have a chat, and

23

then I'll introduce you to Black Bob.'

She showed them into the sitting room, and when they were settled, she began to explain the situation.

'I'm a widow now, and I've decided the best thing is for me to move to Canada so that I can see my family and help with the grandchildren. I need a good home for Bob. He's been a wonderful companion, but at his age I couldn't possibly put him through the stress of such a change.'

As Lynne and Audrey outlined their own circumstances, Lynne could see that Pauline was looking relaxed. When they had finished, she said, 'Come and meet my Bob.'

She led the way to the kitchen, where they saw Bob resting in a basket. He got up stiffly and limped across to them.

'He's got a bit of arthritis,' Pauline explained.

Bob stood in front of them with his head on one side. Audrey bent down and patted him, and he nuzzled her hand.

'He's lovely!' Lynne exclaimed.

Pauline smiled. 'I'm not leaving for a few months, so you've got plenty of time to decide. If you want to go ahead, we can arrange a slow handover.'

'I'm tempted to say yes straight away,' Audrey replied, 'but I think Lynne and I should talk this over and get back to you. If someone else shows an interest, please will you give us first refusal?'

'Of course,' Pauline assured her.

Back at home, Lynne and her mother lay down together on the double bed.

'Now,' Audrey began, 'I definitely want to give that dog a home, but we've got to work out how to go about it. It's a good thing that Pauline is not in any hurry. I think it would be a mistake to bring Bob here before I go into hospital. Have you any news yet about your unpaid leave?'

Lynne hesitated for a second before saying, 'Not really, but I should hear some time next week.'

'What are your thoughts?'

24

'If they say no, I've decided I'm going to hand in my notice.' Lynne held up her hand to stop her mother from speaking. 'Don't say anything. The new manager has cranked up the aggro to a ridiculous extent, and it wouldn't be a bad thing to be out of that place.'

'What will you do instead?' her mother asked anxiously.

'One step at a time, Mum. I'll wait and see what happens next week first, but I've started to think about what I might like to do. There's always temping, I could think of setting up in business myself, or I could do some studying. As I said before, I've got some flexibility because there's equity in my house.'

'But you'll find it difficult to borrow on the strength of that if you're out of work.'

'Don't worry. I'll sort something out.' Lynne laughed, and she felt that a weight was lifting from her. Yes, there were certainly options, and there were bound to be more than she could see at the moment. 'The first step into our future is that you're going to phone on Monday to secure Black Bob. And later I'll fix up his first visit.'

Chapter Five

As Lynne entered her section of the office on Monday morning, she could see something on her desk that looked like yet another letter. This time it was about her lack of commitment to her post. So the news must have filtered through to Lucy about her application for unpaid leave.

She put it in her bag and began work straight away. As was now the norm, her colleagues ignored her presence, but she did not feel upset by this since they did not speak to one another either, and she knew that they were on edge.

She had not worked for long before she became aware of the sound of Lucy's familiar strutting, and it was coming towards her. She did not look up until Lucy half perched on the edge of her desk and said in an inappropriately familiar way, 'I hear that your mother's ill.'

'That's right.'

'And you want special treatment because of that?' she sneered.

'I've applied for unpaid leave so that I can help her when she comes home from hospital.'

Lucy's voice became very quiet. 'Where's your father then?' she mouthed. 'Gone off with someone better?'

Although Lynne had prepared herself for Lucy's tormenting approach once she heard about her mother, she had not for a moment thought that she would stoop so low. She felt as if she had been winded. Lucy was observing her closely, and Lynne did everything she could to conceal her reaction, but Lucy had caught a glimmering of it and seized the opportunity to cause more pain.

'It looks as if your leave won't be granted. I was consulted of course, and I recommended that it shouldn't be granted. Your request was inappropriate, like so much of your behaviour.'

By this time Lynne had tightened her grip on herself, and her initial impulse to knock Lucy off her desk and jump on her had faded.

'Once I have the decision, I'll make the necessary arrangements,' she said coolly.

'Sounds like a funeral,' Lucy remarked nastily. She was clearly irked that she hadn't been able to rile Lynne, and she stalked off.

Lynne discretely took a small bottle out of her handbag, removed the top and passed the bottle under her nose a couple of times. These aromatherapy remedies were invaluable. The scent would not cure the situation, but it filled her mind with something beautiful. Her jangled emotions soothed, she returned her attention to her workload.

It took a considerable amount of determination and application to return to work the next day, but Lynne was determined to meet the challenge. She set off a little earlier than usual so that she would have time to go for a short walk after parking her car.

As she walked, she mentally restated her objectives to herself. Nurse mother, help Black Bob to get used to them, and make plans for the future. These were the things that were important to her, and not the machinations of the diseased mind of Lucy. She could not begin to imagine what prompted such behaviour in her. Lack of confidence leading to overbearing attitudes was one thing, but grade-one bullying was quite another.

When she sat down at her desk, the first thing she did was to check her e-mails. Ah, here was a response to her request for unpaid leave. She opened it and read it. To her surprise, the decision was completely fair. Three weeks unpaid leave had been authorised, and the remaining two weeks had to be taken from her normal leave allocation. It left her with only two days' leave to last her for nearly four months, but that didn't matter. The important thing was that she could tell Mum that she would definitely be the home nurse, and that she still had her job, at least for the time being.

The other surprise of the day was that Lucy was nowhere to be seen. Eventually, news came through that she was off sick, and that no management cover could be provided for the department. As the impact of this percolated the section, people gradually began to speak to one another, and several approached Lynne to ask how she was getting on.

'I'm managing,' she told them. 'Thanks for asking, but I'd better get on now. I've got quite a heavy load to get through before the end of the week.'

The relief of Lucy's absence was palpable, but everyone realised that it would be short-lived, since she was bound to return. If not tomorrow, it would be very soon.

The day passed almost pleasurably.

Once home again, Lynne phoned her mother straight away to tell her the news.

Lucy was back at work the next morning, but she was very subdued, and did not leave her desk.

Despite the overload that Lucy had allocated to her on Monday, Lynne completed nearly all of it by the end of the week, and left work on Friday afternoon with a spring in her step for the first time since Lucy had taken charge.

This was the last weekend that Lynne would have with her mother before the operation, and on Monday, she would deliver her to the hospital on her way to work.

They spent the weekend quietly. They packed and repacked the bag for hospital, checking that everything needed was in it. After that they amused themselves for a while by reading the property pages of the regional newspaper.

'Look at this, Mum!' Lynne exclaimed suddenly as she caught sight of a local property. 'It's in the street just along from mine.'

'Can you read out the details?'

'End terrace. Requires some modernisation. Ground floor:

living room, dining kitchen, bathroom and two bedrooms. Upper floor: two attic rooms. Small garden to front and rear.'

'It's more or less the same as yours, then.'

'That's right. The only difference is that I put a conservatory on the back of mine. It doesn't say anything about heating, so I presume there's nothing in place.'

'What are they asking for it?'

'Mm… It's quite reasonable. Perhaps they're looking for a quick sale. I don't know anyone in that street, so I don't know who it belongs to. Oh, wait a minute… I think that must be the one that's looked empty for quite a while. I used to walk past it when I took Bracken out for an evening stroll. There's a footpath running along the ends of the streets.'

'It's a pity it's come up at the wrong time,' her mother commented.

'What do you mean? Oh! Would you have been interested?'

'I've given your idea of moving closer to you a great deal of thought. This house isn't right for me any more, and I'd be better in one like yours.'

'I'm glad to hear this, Mum. I thought I'd have a long hard job persuading you. Yes, you'd be better off with something like mine, particularly if you were close at hand. And the shops aren't far away either. It's not good here because the shops are a bus ride away. Where I am, even very old people can make their way along to the shops, and *you* aren't very old.'

Lynne's mother sat forward in her chair. 'Lynne, do you think that you could look into this for me?'

'Of course I will. We both know that this isn't the right time for you to be buying and selling, but it's a good opportunity to do a bit of research.'

29

Chapter Six

Lynne stayed overnight with her mother on the Sunday night as they had such an early start on Monday morning. She was to deliver her mother to the hospital around eight, and then she would go straight to work to be ready for a nine o'clock start.

The transfer to hospital went smoothly, and eight fifteen saw Lynne giving her mother a hug and a kiss as she left her saying, 'I'll be in to see you after work, and tomorrow morning is the op.'

Work was an entirely different matter. Lucy was back on form, and had resumed her bullying tactics. Everyone on the floor worked silently, as if each were trapped in an isolated capsule. It was not long before Lynne's antennae sensed that Lucy was setting her course in her direction. Inwardly, she braced herself for the unavoidable onslaught.

'Hello,' said Lucy sweetly.

Lynne looked up from her work. 'Good morning, Lucy,' she replied.

Lucy said nothing, but stared at her in an unpleasant way.

Lynne resumed her work.

'That's impertinent,' Lucy challenged. 'I came to speak to you about your work, and you're ignoring me.'

Lynne looked up again. She said nothing, and waited.

'I see you didn't finish your allocation last week. It's obvious that you were slacking while I was off.'

Lynne thought quickly. She remembered that anything she said could be turned against her, but equally she knew that her silence would be used in the same way.

'I...' she began.

But Lucy broke in. 'There's no excuse, and I shall keep a record of it. You've got quite a list against you now,' she announced triumphantly. Then she flounced off.

Lynne's body remained motionless on her chair, but her other, invisible, self got up and grabbed the back of Lucy's hair and yanked it as hard as she could. That felt *so* good. Lucy spun round. She had obviously sensed something, but when she saw that Lynne had not moved from her seat, she shook her head momentarily and then continued in the direction in which she was already moving.

Lynne found that her work seemed much easier after that, and by five o'clock she had finished the end of last week's work and was well into the first section of this week's. She went to the toilets and locked herself in a cubicle for a good fifteen minutes before leaving. As she had hoped, Lucy was nowhere to be seen.

At the hospital, she was glad to find that her mother looked calm and relaxed.

'The anaesthetist came round to see me this afternoon,' she said. 'He was very helpful.'

Lynne blessed the turn of events that had sent that particular person on that day.

Her mother went on. 'I'm second on the list in the morning. That means I don't have to wait a long time, thinking about what's going to happen.'

'That's good news,' said Lynne. 'And remember, soon we'll be phoning Pauline again about Black Bob.'

'I was speaking to one of the nurses about him earlier today. She told me that there's a homeopathic remedy that can sometimes help with arthritis in dogs. I'll get her to write it down for me, and we can try it on Bob.'

Lynne noticed a pink glow on her mother's drawn face. What more confirmation did she need that they were making the right decision about Bob? 'I won't stay long this evening, Mum,' she said, 'and of course I'll be back tomorrow. I'll phone the ward at lunchtime to find out how things have gone.'

'Do you know, Lynne, I feel quite excited. I was very anxious after I got my diagnosis, but now I feel quite differently.

31

I've got a sense that this is a gateway to the future.'

'Yes, *our* future,' Lynne whispered softly as she kissed her mother goodbye.

On her way out of the ward, she turned and saw her mother watching her leave. They waved to each other, and then Lynne turned down the corridor towards the exit door.

She went to bed early that night, and was surprised to find that she slept very well.

The following morning she rose early, and was in the office well before nine. This gave her time to arrange her desk and begin her work promptly.

'Trying to catch up, are we?' Lucy sneered as she clicked past on ridiculously high heels.

Lynne acted as if she had heard nothing, and continued her work.

Lucy returned. 'Your mother's *really* ill, isn't she?' she said in a low voice.

Lynne's body kept working, while her invisible self stuck two invisible pens up Lucy's nostrils.

'Ow!' Lucy squawked, grabbing her nose. She rushed to the cloakroom to examine herself in the mirror, but seeing nothing, she returned to pester Lynne.

Lynne hated the heavy smell of her perfume. It was entirely unsuitable for an office environment, and it left her feeling that she was being suffocated.

'Your mummy won't be at home to make your tea for you,' Lucy chanted, in nasal tones. She was careful to ensure that no one else could hear what she was saying. In fact, had anyone taken any notice, it would have looked as if Lucy were helping Lynne with her work.

Lynne was determined that Lucy would not get the better of her. Silently, she repeated over and over in her mind 'I'm fine'. It seemed to work, because she certainly felt fine. She felt relaxed and entirely in charge of herself and her life. Lucy was behaving like a silly little girl who was taking out her feelings –

probably about her own lack of parenting – on someone else, in a 'playground' setting. Lynne filled her mind with thoughts of how at lunchtime she would phone the hospital and learn that her mother's operation had gone well.

Lucy gave up and went to her desk, where she spent the next half hour polishing her nails, before being called away to a meeting. Lynne barely noticed her leave, as she was devising a plan whereby she could phone the hospital without interruption.

The morning sped by, and soon it was time for her lunch break. Swiftly she picked up her bag, went to her car, and drove to the car park of the supermarket that was only a few hundred yards down the road. She took out her mobile, and direct-dialled the ward.

'This is Lynne Fenton. I'm phoning to ask how my mother is.'

'She's doing fine,' came the reply. 'There were no complications.'

'Thanks. Give her my love.'

'I will.'

Lynne rang off, ate the sandwich she had brought with her that day, and then returned to the office as quickly as she could. Mercifully, Lucy had not been aware of her absence. Lynne felt confident that she would have dealt with the consequences, but it was a pleasant relief to find that there was no need. The afternoon passed without interruption, and Lynne concentrated well on her work, secure in the knowledge that her mother would soon be on the mend.

She visited the hospital only briefly, as her mother was still sleepy from the anaesthetic and the painkillers. Back home, she phoned Sarah.

As soon as Sarah heard Lynne's voice, she asked, 'How's your mum?'

'Everything's going well. She had her op today, and there are no complications.'

'I'm very glad to hear that. I've never met her, but do give her my love and say that I'm thinking about her.'

'Thanks, I will.'

'How are things at work?'

'Pretty mixed. I applied for five weeks of unpaid leave so that I can nurse Mum when she comes home. Although Lucy tried to block it, I've been given three unpaid, and the rest I have to take out of my paid leave, which I think is fair.'

'I'd agree with that.'

'Lucy's behaviour is pretty off-the-wall. I won't bore you with details. The curious thing is that as time goes on I'm less affected by it. I've decided that if she somehow engineers that I lose my job, it won't be the end of the world. There's far more to life than that. I can see now that there's something wrong with her, and that anything I do or say isn't going to change it.'

'I'm relieved to hear you say all of that.'

'I'm noticing that I'm even managing to more or less keep up with the entirely unrealistic workload that she's putting on me.'

Sarah burst out laughing. 'Well done! That'll give her something to think about. I expect she was hoping that you'd crack under the strain, particularly if she knows your mother's not well.'

'That's what I thought too. How are things with you, Sarah?'

'I've got some repairs to the house to see to, but apart from that everything's going okay. The children are looking after themselves more and more. The oldest has flown the nest, and I don't think it'll be too long before the others follow.'

'Andy's left home already?'

'He's turned eighteen, you know.'

'What's he doing?'

'He's moved into a shared flat and is continuing his training to be a plumber. He's loving every minute of it.'

'The best of luck to him. We're needing some good plumbers.'

'I'll tell him. Now, remember to let me know how your mother gets on.'

34

Lynne put the phone down. She felt enriched by her conversation with Sarah. How sad for someone like Lucy that she was incapable of taking part in an interaction that was helpful to both people, instead of damaging both herself and others by whatever was affecting her. Sarah had not had an easy time. Her husband had died when her boys were young, and she had brought them up single-handed.

Lynne didn't feel particularly hungry, so she made herself a sandwich with a nutritious filling, and settled for that. It was as she was finishing the last mouthful that she remembered she had not yet phoned for more details of the house for sale on the next row. Then she realised that she could probably access them from the internet, and she switched on her computer.

Soon she was viewing pictures of the rooms, and could see immediately that there was quite a lot of work to be done. Since pictures always tried to convey the best, it must be the case that the property was in poor shape, she thought. Then an idea struck her. She checked the time. Eight thirty. Although viewing was by appointment only, she could go round and see if anyone was there. Why not?

A few minutes later, she was standing outside the house, but she knew straight away that there would be no one inside. A neighbour across the road was weeding his garden, and Lynne asked him if he knew anything about it.

'An elderly gent used to live there, but he was taken into a care home last year. The house was pretty run down by then, and things haven't improved. Pulls down the tone of the neighbourhood rather. You interested?'

'My mother might be. Do you know how to contact the owner?'

'Well, as a matter of fact I've a number to ring if I see any problems with the roof. I offered to keep an eye open when they took the owner away. Don't know whose number it is, though. I've never had cause to use it. The roof's the one thing that seems okay.'

'Could you let me have the number?'

'Just a minute.' The man wiped his hands on the small grassed area, and disappeared inside his house. When he returned, he handed a slip of paper to Lynne. 'Here it is. Just say I gave it to you. My name's Bert Gray.'

'Thanks very much,' said Lynne, and she retraced her steps.

Once back home, she decided on impulse to phone the number to see what she could find out. A woman answered, and when Lynne explained why she had rung, the woman told her, 'It'll be my husband you'll need to speak to. His dad died, and now he's beginning to sort things out. He'll be in before ten. I can get him to give you a ring.'

Lynne left her name and number, and then found herself wandering aimlessly around her house. When she realised what she was doing, she felt irritated with herself. However, she soon accepted that she had nothing else she wanted to do with her time while she waited to see if the owner would contact her.

Ten came and went, and Lynne had almost given up hope of hearing anything that evening, when the phone rang.

'Lynne Fenton?'

'Speaking.'

'This is Thomas Brown. I'm the owner of number twenty, Primrose Terrace. How can I help you?'

'I'm at twenty, Bluebell Terrace. My mother is hoping to move to be nearer to me, and we saw that your property is for sale. I was hoping to arrange a time to view it.'

'I'm coming across tomorrow evening, seven 'til nine. Will that suit?'

'That'll be fine for me. I'll be with you some time after eight.'

Chapter Seven

When Lynne saw her mother after work the next day, she was looking tired, but surprisingly well for someone who had so recently undergone surgery.

'They say there's a chance I might be discharged on Saturday morning.'

'That would be perfect. I can get some food in and then come and collect you, and we can have a cosy weekend together. You can have plenty of rest, and I'll keep making small meals for you.'

'You don't need to take that much trouble.'

'I've been finding out about aftercare, and my instinct was right. Those who nurse their digestive system well after surgery have the best results. So, you'll just have to accept my plans.'

Her mother looked at her gratefully. 'It's made such a difference to me to know that you'll be with me. I won't have to worry about asking people for things, and we'll have lots of time together to chat and to talk about the future. It's everything I would have wanted.'

'I've got some news about one of our plans,' Lynne announced.

'What is it?'

'I'm going to see that house when I get home this evening. Don't worry, I won't commit us to anything. It's only the start of our researches.'

'I'll look forward to hearing all about it tomorrow.'

Lynne noticed that her mother was beginning to look very weary. 'I think that's enough excitement for today,' she said firmly. 'I'm off now, but I'll see you very soon. Sleep well.' She kissed her mother's cheek, and made her way out of the hospital.

Once home, she changed into some jeans and a shirt, and again made a sandwich for herself. It was nearly eight by the time she was ready. She felt a sense of anticipation as she set off on the short walk round to 20 Primrose Terrace.

There was no bell push and no knocker, so she banged the side of her fist on the door a few times. At first there was no response, and she was considering whether or not to come back later, when she heard a sound in the hall. The door was opened by a thin man, who looked to be in his late fifties or early sixties.

'Mr Brown? I'm Lynne Fenton.' She held out her hand. His handshake conveyed friendship, although despite it being summertime, his bony fingers seemed quite cold.

'Do come in. I'm afraid it's a bit of a mess in here. I've put off doing the clearing up, but now I can't avoid it any longer. And my wife's not too well.'

'My mother's in hospital at the moment,' Lynne told him. 'That's why she can't come to look for herself.'

'I see.' He allowed himself to digest this information, and then said, 'Your house must be much the same as this.'

'Yes, although I do have a conservatory at the back. I added it last year.'

'The attic rooms are accessed only by ladder here.'

'That's another difference, then,' Lynne commented. 'I have a narrow staircase that leads up to mine.'

Mr Brown showed her into the front room. The walls were heavily stained from years of exposure to tobacco smoke, the furniture was threadbare, the carpet square had holes in it and the grate was full of ash. He looked at her apologetically, but said nothing, and then led her to the kitchen and dining area. Here, she saw only bare boards, an ancient cooker and an old-fashioned ceramic sink.

'My father refused to have any modern appliances,' Mr Brown explained. 'I'll show you the bedrooms.'

The bedroom that looked out to the back contained the frame of a single bed, whereas the other bedroom had a wardrobe, chest of drawers and a double bed.

There was a ladder in the hallway, and Mr Brown extended it to reach the hatch in the ceiling. 'I'll leave you to go up and look,' he told her, 'I can't stand heights.'

Lynne cautiously tried the first few rungs. The ladder seemed quite stable, so she climbed the rest of the height quite confidently, lifted the hatch and looked in. She gasped involuntarily when she saw what was there. The doors of the two rooms were open, and she could see that the whole of the attic space was filled with piles of books.

She went back down the ladder and said, 'I don't think I need to go into the attic. I can see that apart from not having velux windows, the two rooms are similar to the ones in my own house.'

'My father was a booklover,' Mr Brown explained unnecessarily.

Lynne said nothing. She could not imagine why a booklover would put all his books in the most inaccessible part of the house and leave them there.

Mr Brown continued. 'My mother didn't like books. She said they were pretentious. So my father kept them in the attic. By the time my mother died, he was long past the stage where he could get them down, and I've never liked heights myself, so I couldn't help.' He paused, and then added. 'He didn't want anyone else in the house.'

'That's a shame,' said Lynne. She couldn't think of anything else to say about it, so asked to see the bathroom.

Mr Brown winced. 'I'm afraid it needs a lot of attention.'

Lynne went to the bathroom door and opened it to reveal a mess. She was glad to have had some prior warning of its state. The floor was rotted, the sink, bath and toilet were a hideous green colour and were cracked and stained, and there was a strange smell. She shut the door again.

'Er... I see what you mean,' she agreed. 'When are you hoping to have the house sold by?'

Here Mr Brown surprised her by saying, 'To be honest with

you, it's been on the market for weeks, and you're the first person to come and see it. As I said, my wife doesn't keep too well, and the whole thing's a bit much for me.'

'Why not put it in the hands of someone who'll do all the work for you?' Lynne suggested.

Mr Brown looked at his shoes, and then confided, 'I don't want to do that. My father hated interference. It would be disrespectful.'

'I think I understand,' said Lynne sympathetically. 'Since you've been so good as to tell me something of your circumstances, maybe I should tell you a little more of mine. My mother will take a while to recover from the operation she had earlier this week, so we won't be able to put her house on the market for a while. I'll be seeing her again tomorrow after work, and I'll talk to her about this house. Could I give you a ring some time over the next few days?'

'Surely.'

He let her out into the street, where she blinked in the evening light. Somehow it seemed rather bright.

Chapter Eight

Lucy's campaign of unpleasantness and harassment continued largely unabated, but it barely penetrated Lynne's consciousness. Her mind was completely taken up with finishing off her work, and the five weeks beyond that beckoned. In the fragments of time when she became aware of Lucy, she could see that she was annoyed that her ploys were not having the desired effect, and she wondered if Lucy would move on to someone else during the time she would not be there to target.

After work, she hurried to the hospital to find her mother waiting eagerly for news of the house.

'What was it like, Lynne?' she asked.

'To be honest it was a bit of a mess. The bathroom will have to be entirely replaced – floorboards and all. There's no kitchen to speak of, the attic can only be reached by a ladder, and there's no heating apart from a couple of open fires. But I've been thinking.'

'Tell me what's in your mind.'

'There were various things Mr Brown said that leave me thinking that he might be open to a private deal, and that he might not be in any particular hurry to sell. I think the most important thing to him is to have the right buyer.'

Her mother leaned forward from her pillows. 'What makes you think that?'

Lynne recounted everything that had happened.

'I see what you mean,' said her mother slowly. Lynne saw excitement in her eyes as she added, 'Do you think we might have a chance?'

'We could see,' Lynne replied. 'Although you're going to be recuperating, with the five weeks we're going to have together, it's going to be a lot easier to follow this up. Anyway, one step at a time. Tomorrow we'll find out if you're getting out on Saturday. If everything goes according to plan, I'll arrange Bob's first visit towards the end of next week, and once we've thought through this house business, I'll phone Mr Brown again. I must say, I'm tempted to send a surveyor round to see how a valuation compares with the advertised price.'

'At the moment, the thought of selling my house seems too difficult.'

'Of course it will,' Lynne sympathised. 'But I'm sure we can find ways round it if we decide to go ahead. However, we're just toying with ideas at the moment. Now,' she added briskly, 'that's enough for today. I'll see you tomorrow.'

At the end of the following day, Lynne risked Lucy's wrath by saying goodbye to all her colleagues, explaining that she was going to look after her mother, and would return in five weeks' time. Lucy disappeared into the cloakroom with a sulky look on her face, and Lynne received a very warm response from everyone else, as they all wished her and her mother well.

She had difficulty in restraining herself from skipping across the car park. She felt happy. No, not just happy, joyful. She and her mother were embarking on an adventure.

When she arrived at the hospital, Audrey was sitting in an easy chair beside her bed. She tried to stand up, but found it difficult.

'Drat,' she grumbled. 'I was on my feet earlier.'

'Be patient, Mum. You'll get your energy back. What's the news for tomorrow?'

'I've been told that if you come about noon, I'll be ready to leave.'

'Oh, Mum!' Lynne exclaimed excitedly. 'I thought that would be the news, but I couldn't be absolutely certain.'

'Can you phone Pauline before you come to get me?' asked her mother anxiously.

'I think we should leave it until you're settled at home.

You'll be surprised how much it'll take out of you just making the change back from hospital. I'll phone her sometime next week.'

They spent the rest of the visit making a shopping list, so that Lynne could buy everything they would need for two or three days.

When Lynne went home, she packed a bag ready to take to her mother's, and then she phoned Sarah.

'How's everything?' Sarah asked.

'Mum's coming on really well. I'm to collect her tomorrow.'

'That's such good news! How was work?'

'Fine. I don't know how it'll be when I go back, but that's a long time away. I hope Lucy doesn't start on someone else, though.'

'I'm afraid that's exactly the kind of thing that might happen,' Sarah commented.

'I wanted to leave Mum's number with you, in case you want to phone me there,' said Lynne.

'Good idea. Hang on, I'll get something to write on.'

Sarah copied down the number, and finished the call by saying, 'I'll speak to you some time soonish.'

Chapter Nine

Lynne was awake very early. She lay in bed until seven, but after that she felt restless, and she got up, breakfasted, and was at the supermarket for eight. It was wonderfully quiet at that time, and shopping was a pleasure, especially as everything she bought was for her and her mother to share.

She took the shopping to her mother's house, and stacked it in the cupboards. Then she opened all the windows for an hour or so to air the house. She put fresh sheets on her mother's bed, and she loaded the others into the washing machine. There was enough time to finish the cycle and put them out on the line, before setting off to the hospital.

She parked her car as near to the exit as possible. When she arrived on the ward, her mother was sitting near the nursing station, with everything ready packed. Soon they were driving home.

'I wish I could go to see at least the outside of that house,' said her mother, her voice full of longing.

'And I wish I could take you,' replied Lynne, 'but it would be foolish. However, it's a good sign that you feel you want to.'

'Yes, my mind's been filling up with all kinds of things I want to do. I can see now that I'd been waiting to see how the operation went before I could really believe I had some life ahead of me. But Lynne, I don't think it's feasible to go ahead with anything definite about that house. It's too soon.'

'I agree, but it's been good to think about it. I'm sure that something else will come up later. I'll phone Mr Brown on Monday and let him know we can't take things any further.'

By the time they were back at her house, Audrey was exhausted.

'You were right about the change from hospital to home,'

she said. 'I'll have to go straight to bed.'

'That's what I'd planned. Everything's ready for you.'

They spent the weekend very quietly. As promised, Lynne made regular small meals for her mother, who spent much of her time in bed, sometimes reading, sometimes dozing and sometimes chatting. One of the neighbours called round with a bunch of mixed flowers, but she declined Lynne's invitation to come in for a cup of tea.

'I'll come in later on,' she promised. 'Audrey won't feel up to much yet, and I expect you'll be popping in and out as the days go on. I'll come and sit with her for a while when you're out and about.'

Monday came, and Lynne phoned Mr Brown. He did not sound surprised about her decision, and said that he hoped her mother was progressing well. Lynne relayed this to her mother.

'What a kind man!' her mother exclaimed. 'And he doesn't even know me.'

'Yes, I must say that although the house was in a bit of a state, I took to him,' said Lynne.

Later in the week, Lynne arranged to collect Bob from Pauline's.

'I've an old blanket in the cupboard on the landing that you can put for Bob on the back seat of your car,' Audrey told her. 'And I'm going to be downstairs to welcome him.'

'Are you sure?' asked Lynne.

'I'm certain. I'll come down before you leave.'

Lynne was soon on her way to collect Bob.

'That's a lovely lead,' Pauline commented as she let Lynne in.

'I saw it in the pet shop on Saturday morning and had to buy it. I was really struck by the number of bright colours that are woven through it.'

After drinking a cup of tea with Pauline, Lynne led Bob to her car. He hesitated when she opened the door to the back seat, and turned his head to look at her.

'Good boy,' she encouraged. 'Go on.' She gave him a gentle push, and he climbed in and settled himself on the blanket. 'Good boy,' she repeated. 'Now, I'm going to take you home to my mum's house. You'll like it there.'

She waved goodbye to Pauline, and then turned to look at Bob. She was reassured to see that he was curled up on the blanket, looking intently at her. She drove quite slowly at first. Bob did not move, and she increased her speed.

Once back at her mother's house, she helped him out of the car. It was obvious that his legs were painful, and she saw to it that they were not jarred. She led him into the house.

'Welcome home, Bob,' said Audrey, patting his head. Bob licked her fingers. 'Lynne, there's an old rug in the garage that he can have. I should have asked you to bring it in this morning.'

'Never mind, it won't be damp in this weather. You take Bob, and I'll get it for him straight away.'

Lynne put the rug near the door of the sitting room, and left it ajar so that he could go into the kitchen for water if he was thirsty. She showed him where she had put the bowl of water, and then he followed her to the sitting room. He went to his rug straight away, and flopped down on it.

'He looks a bit like I feel,' Audrey remarked, laughing. 'Bob, I think you and I are going to get on very well together.' She turned to Lynne. 'If you look in the writing-case I had with me in hospital, you'll see the name of the remedy that the nurse suggested for Bob. Would you put it on the shopping list?'

'Of course I will. Perhaps I should pop out now for it.'

Her mother looked nervous. 'I'd rather you left it until another day. I have to admit that I felt a bit wobbly when you were away picking Bob up.'

'I'm glad you told me,' Lynne replied. 'I can't tell from just looking at you.'

Bob's first visit had gone very well, and more were arranged.

Lynne was pleased to see that her two charges were progressing. Each day, her mother gained a little strength, and each day, Bob became more confident. At first he was quite timid, and she had to offer food and water and time in the garden, but after another few visits, he had begun to push at her hand with his nose if there was anything that he wanted.

'I think he's coming along quite nicely,' Audrey observed one day. 'And that medicine seems to be having some kind of effect. I think he's not limping so badly.'

'Yes, Pauline noticed that, too. She was so pleased and very grateful. Maybe I'll try taking him out for a short walk soon.'

'Yes, he's gaining confidence now, so you could give it a try.'

'Would you like to come too?' asked Lynne. 'We could go a little way in one direction and then come back and go the other way.'

'What a good idea. Yes, I'd like to give it a try.'

After a hundred yards in one direction, Audrey was ready to turn back. Bob seemed happy to be out, so they agreed that they would go home, and then Lynne would try taking him for a longer walk.

But on her return, she met her mother coming to meet them.

'You shouldn't be out on your own,' Lynne chided.

'I'm fine. After you'd gone I worked out that I wasn't tired. It was my confidence that was the problem. I've been walking up and down in front of the house, and I feel much better for it. From now on, I'll be going for a short walk every day. I want to get my strength up so that we can enjoy some outings together while you're off work.'

'I want that too, but don't rush at it and push yourself backwards.'

'Don't worry, I'll be careful.'

Over a cup of tea, Lynne made a suggestion. 'Shall we try going to the supermarket together tomorrow? We don't need to be out for long, and we can see how you manage.'

'That's a good idea. And we'll have to work out how to go shopping when we have Bob with us. He won't be able to come into the shops, and we've never left him before.'

'That's a good point.'

Then Audrey's face lit up. 'I've had an idea. You could drive us all to the supermarket car park, and then I can sit with Bob in the car. He should be all right if I'm there.'

Chapter Ten

Two more weeks passed, during which the length and frequency of their modest outings increased.

'That's three of my weeks gone already,' Lynne realised one afternoon. 'Never mind, though. You and Bob are much more mobile now, and we'll keep on having a good time together.'

Audrey took a deep breath. 'Lynne, I've been thinking about that house again.'

'You mean 20 Primrose Terrace?'

'Yes. As I've been getting my strength back, I'm beginning to feel that I could go ahead with a move.'

'We mustn't rush it,' Lynne warned. 'You were right not to push ahead when I'd seen that house.'

'Yes, but now I'd like to find out more about it. That is, if it's still on the market.'

'Okay,' Lynne agreed. 'I think I kept the phone number somewhere. Shall I give Mr Brown a ring, and we'll take it from there?'

There was no reply, and Lynne left a message on the answering service, giving her mother's phone number.

'What exactly have you got in mind?' she asked when she replaced the phone.

'If it's still on the market, I'd like to have a look at it. Its location couldn't be better, but obviously it's in pretty bad condition. The big questions will be to do with whether or not I can face sorting out all its problems, and how I'd go about the sale of this house.'

'Well, your house is in very good condition,' Lynne pointed out. 'I would say there's nothing to be done to it before you try to sell it, and in our situation that's a huge bonus.'

'Yes, I've kept on doing a bit to it every year or so, although it's been mostly out of respect for your dad. He kept it so nice when he was alive. Lynne, did you say that Sarah's son is training to be a plumber?'

'That's right.'

'If I do get the house, maybe he'll be able to do some of the work.'

'I never thought about that, but you're right. I'll ask Sarah when I speak to her again.'

'Obviously I'll need to find the money to buy the house and put it to rights before I can move from here. That's a big stumbling block. I've got some capital, but it won't be enough. I think I should go and see a financial advisor. I need some guidance about who to approach about a loan.'

Lynne smiled. 'Well, there's always the option of putting your things into storage, and moving in with me. Actually, I'd rather like that. These last three weeks have been a kind of holiday. It's been lovely to have the three of us together, and when I go home it's going to feel really strange.'

Just then, the phone rang. Audrey picked it up.

'Hello? Oh, yes, Mr Brown ... Yes, this is Mrs Fenton ... Thank you, I'm feeling much better. I hear that your wife hasn't been well ... Ah, she's a bit better ... I'm glad to hear it. My daughter and I wanted to know if 20 Primrose Terrace is still for sale ... It is? Could we arrange to come and see it? Yes ... we're pretty flexible at the moment ... Tomorrow afternoon at two? That would be perfect. Thank you, we'll see you then.' She put down the phone and turned to Lynne. 'You'll have gathered what he said.'

Lynne nodded. 'And if when you've seen it you want to go ahead, we'll put some wheels in motion.'

'Why don't we make a start now?'

'But there's no point.'

'There's *every* point,' her mother corrected her.

Astonished, Lynne stared at her. There was an energy and enthusiasm coming from her that Lynne had not seen since before her dad died. 'Mum, you look great!' she exclaimed. 'But I still don't follow what you mean.'

'I'll phone the solicitor that dealt with Frank's will.'

'But that's fifteen years ago, the firm might not even exist now,' Lynne pointed out.

'I happen to know that the firm's still there, but of course the solicitor might not be. Now... what was his name?' Audrey was thoughtful for a few minutes and then said, 'Bragg. That's it! Malcolm Bragg at Jenkins and Bragg.'

'They might not handle property.'

Audrey looked at her daughter with an exasperated expression. 'If they don't, I can ask them to recommend someone. What's the matter, Lynne? Is something wrong?'

Lynne looked at her mother, bemused. 'You'll have to give me time to get used to the new you,' she explained. 'I remember you being like this when I used to live at home, but certainly not since Dad died.'

Her mother stopped and reflected. 'I always believed I'd managed to hide it from you. The heart just went out of this house when your dad died. I did my best to carry on, but it wasn't the same.'

'I wish you'd talked to me about it.'

'I didn't want to do anything that might hold you back. I was worried that if I said something, you might feel you had to spend time with me that you needed to use elsewhere.'

Lynne took in what her mother was saying and felt its impact very strongly.

'Oh, no!' she said. 'I can see it now. I wish I could have put something into words at the time. Mum, this might be why I chose that awful man. Because neither of us could talk about our loss, I ended up trying to get a replacement, and made a terrible mess of it!'

Her mother looked very upset.

Lynne continued. 'Now, don't go blaming yourself. Like I said before, I was an adult woman, responsible for my own life.'

Her mother wiped a tear from the corner of her eye. 'We've

got to make something good out of this,' she said determinedly. 'Lynne, I read an article about ill-health in a magazine when I was in hospital.'

Lynne groaned. 'But that kind of thing is usually so superficial.'

'I know, and I was surprised when I found that this one was worth reading. Actually, it was a piece that had been written by someone who had spent time at a cancer help centre. You know, the kind of place that looks at illness from a lot of different angles. The point that really made an impression on me was the need to look at relationships. I'd always rather taken mine for granted. I'd always loved being round people, and helping where I could. But after Frank died, without really noticing, I'd gradually withdrawn more and more. Oh, I still went to work, and I still saw people, but there was a kind of distance between me and the life around me. I don't think anyone would have noticed, and I could only see it myself after I read the article. But I'm now certain it was something that contributed to my becoming ill.'

'Mm, that's very interesting,' Lynne mused. 'If you're right, that's how I got the impression you wanted time on your own, and for me to get on with my life. Well, we're not going to make any of these mistakes again. We're going to talk a lot about Dad and how much we've missed him, and then if I find someone for myself, it won't be for the wrong reasons. And by the way, I think you should phone that solicitor straight away.'

Audrey picked up the phone book, and was soon speaking to someone at Jenkins and Bragg.

When she put the phone down, she announced, 'Malcolm Bragg has retired, but the firm has a large property department, with a specialist solicitor in charge of it. I'll definitely use that firm. Lynne, are you quite sure about your offer that I can live with you for a while?'

'Of course I am, Mum. It would be lovely to have you and Bob.'

'Well, I think I should get back to Jenkins and Bragg very

soon, to put this house on the market.'

Lynne and her mother arrived at the gate of 20 Primrose Terrace, just after two. The sun was shining on the little patch of garden at the front, and Mr Brown was sitting on a rickety wooden chair, dozing in the heat. Lynne spoke to him gently, and he jerked awake. She noticed that his face brightened when he saw them.

'I'm glad you've come,' he said unguardedly. It was as if he had expected that they might not appear. He held out his hand and shook Audrey's, saying, 'Mrs Fenton, do come in. I expect your daughter will have explained my situation.'

Audrey nodded. 'Yes, I understand that there's work needing to be done.'

'Perhaps you and your daughter would like time to look round on your own?' he asked. 'I can wait here in the garden, and you can fetch me if there's anything you want to know.'

Lynne was grateful for this suggestion. 'That's very helpful. Is that okay with you, Mum?'

Audrey agreed, and they made their way into the sitting room at the front. The sun was trying its best to force a way through the dirt on the window panes, and the room seemed cold.

'This room needs a bit of love and attention,' Audrey remarked. 'Let's see the rest.'

'It gets worse,' Lynne warned.

She took her mother round the rest of the ground floor, finishing with the bathroom.

'Mm, I see what you mean,' Audrey agreed. 'But I stand by what I said. It all needs a bit of love and attention.'

'A *lot* of love, I'd say,' Lynne corrected her, laughing. 'By the way, I'm not letting you up the ladder today. You'll have to take my word for what it's like up there.'

They lingered in the hallway for a few minutes.

'There's enough garden for Bob,' said Lynne. 'But what do you think, Mum? There's a huge amount of work to be done.

You'll have to do most of the arranging – if I've still got a job when I turn up for work.'

'I want to be daring,' her mother replied. 'Life is for living. I know that now. I want to settle here. Let's tell Mr Brown that I'm interested.'

The look of relief on Thomas Brown's face was worth a photograph, Lynne thought as she watched her mother speaking to him.

'I'll get a surveyor round as soon as I can, and we can take it from there,' Audrey told him. 'And don't worry, if we make a deal, we can come to some arrangement about the removal of the books from the loft.'

'I would very much like you to have my father's house,' said Mr Brown, with the same lack of caution that he had showed earlier.

As they left, a well-built man appeared out of the front door of number eighteen, holding the hand of a small child. He waved cheerfully to them as they passed his gate. Both were wearing brightly-coloured shirts that reminded Lynne of a tropical island. She and her mother waved back, and the child called, 'Hi!'

Back in the car, Lynne said, 'I've always admired colours like that.'

'Why not buy something really bright for yourself?' her mother suggested.

Lynne looked at her with surprise. 'But... but you wouldn't ever consider wearing anything like that yourself,' she protested.

'That doesn't mean that *you* shouldn't. Look, I'm a bit tired now, but maybe we can go clothes shopping one day before you have to go back to work.'

After that day, things moved very quickly. The surveyor's report for 20 Primrose Terrace revealed that despite everything Lynne and her mother had already noted, everything else about the house was sound. Audrey put in an offer for it, and Mr Brown accepted it straight away. By this time, Jenkins and

Bragg had put a 'For Sale' notice up in her own front garden, and already people were making enquiries.

'I can hardly believe how quickly this all seems to be falling into place,' said Audrey after they had showed a young couple out of the front door.

'Yes, I think we'll put off that clothes shopping trip for now. We've got too much to get on with. I should give Sarah a ring to ask if Andy will be able to do some plumbing work, and we'll need to get more tradespeople lined up.'

'Lynne, I've been putting a lot of thought into that.'

'What are you planning?'

'Having thought about Andy, it's been in my mind to give some more young people a chance of work, and I've got two ideas. We could try to get some contacts through the Prince's Trust, or...'

'Or what?'

'I want to look into using youngsters who've been in the Young Offenders Institution. Do you remember that course I went on about crime and punishment?'

'Of course I do. It was a few years ago though.'

'I saw round that prison as part of the course, and I was impressed by the workshops they had, where the young people could learn about certain trades. There was quite a section on painting and decorating, for example.'

'I think I'm beginning to follow you.'

'There were some halfway houses on the prison perimeter, where young people lived and worked from near the end of their term. Lynne, I'd like to make some enquiries. Your dad and I never had a son of our own, and this would be a way of giving a helping hand to some young people who are trying to make something of their lives.'

Lynne was enthusiastic. 'I'm with you now. I think it's a great idea. And if it means that the work takes a bit longer, that's all to the good.'

'What do you mean?'

'You'll be with me while you're waiting,' Lynne reminded

her. She checked her watch. 'Sarah should be in now. I'll give her a ring to let her know what we're doing, and she can ask Andy if he can do some work for us.'

Soon she was deep in conversation with Sarah.

'That's such good news,' said Sarah. 'Your mum sounds as if she's coming along really quickly. And the house you've found sounds just the job, given that she can stay with you while it's being sorted out.'

'Yes, we're very excited about it. Mum's house is already on the market, and quite few people have been to see it. On the front of sorting out the house we're getting, I wanted to ask you if Andy might be interested in doing some of the work.'

'Remember that he's only able to do plumbing.'

Lynne chuckled. 'We'll need quite a bit of that. The bathroom and the kitchen are both disaster areas. And there's another thing. If he's willing to take some of it on, he won't need to rush at it if Mum's with me.'

'Sounds an interesting proposition. And I've had another thought. He's got a friend who's recently finished his training as an electrician and he's trying to build up a small business for himself. Do you want me to ask about him?'

'Perfect! We're taking possession of the house in a couple of months' time, and it would be a very good thing to get some of this organised before then. Mum's keen to get young people involved, hoping that it will help to give them a start.'

'I like that idea. I'll get on to Andy as soon as I can. Can I give him your mum's number?'

'Of course.' Lynne rang off and said to her mother, 'Fingers crossed that we get a plumber and an electrician out of that phone call.'

'Oh good! Lynne, I've read so much about solar panels recently that I'm determined to have some fitted on the roof. And I've made up my mind that I'm definitely going to get the painting and decorating done by young men who are trying to get back into society.'

'I like the way you're making all these decisions, Mum, and

I think you're absolutely right in what you're planning. Oh, I wish I didn't have to go back to work next week!'

'It may not be a bad thing,' her mother replied. 'I'm more or less on my feet now, and I can get on with all of this while you see how things are working out with your employment.'

'Yes, I suppose it's time to go and see what Lucy's been up to in my absence,' Lynne acknowledged, 'and if it's all bad news, I might well go for a change of career.'

To their surprise and delight, an offer for the house came in just before the weekend. It was from a young couple with a baby. They were moving from a rented flat, and this was to be their first real home.

'It couldn't be better,' said Audrey. 'It makes it so much easier for me to part with this house, if I know it's going to a young family. I'll say that they can move in whenever they want.'

'I don't think that would be sensible,' Lynne cautioned her.

'Why ever not?'

'You've got to think of getting yourself ready to move. At the very least, you've got to have time to sort out what you need to bring with you to my house, and what to put in store.'

'You're right, of course. I was thinking only of their happiness and not of the practicalities.'

'In any case, they'll have to give notice on their flat. Let's wait and find out what date will be best all round.'

Chapter Eleven

When Lynne arrived at work, she was surprised to find that the rest of her team looked happy and relaxed. When they saw her, they all came over to greet her.

'Welcome back,' said Damien, a young man who was one of the more recent recruits.

'How's your mum?' asked Carol, the most senior member of the team.

'She's fine, thanks,' Lynne replied. 'She's so much better than she was. It's almost as if she's a different person.' Inwardly, she reflected that this was not just a useful phrase to use, and that in some ways it was actually true. 'Where's Lucy?' she added cautiously.

Carol explained. 'She handed in her notice the week after you went off. She finished on Friday.'

Lynne was astonished. 'Why?' she asked incredulously.

'It's all a bit of a mystery,' Carol replied. 'And now we're waiting to see who's going to replace her. We've all agreed that we work better without her than with her, so we're not worried about how long it'll take. How about you?'

Lynne grinned. 'I must admit it's a huge relief. It'll be good to get back to helping each other again. The imposed lack of communication wasn't a good thing at all.'

Later that morning, Carol was called out to a meeting. She returned during the coffee break.

'Is there any news?' Lynne asked her.

'I'm to take responsibility for the team until they decide what to do.'

Lynne was ecstatic. 'That's great news! Let's tell the others.'

The response was much the same as Lynne's had been, and

Damien held his cup in the air, proclaiming, 'Here's to a better future for us all!'

Everyone was in a relaxed mood as they drifted away from the group, back to their desks.

Carol continued her conversation with Lynne. 'I've been doing a bit of research since we hit the problem with Lucy, and not only have I heard that this kind of thing is rife in some offices, but also that the way complaints procedures are followed can be flawed.'

Lynne shuddered. 'I certainly felt that Lucy was bending the complaints procedure to suit herself, and that no one was stopping her. Creating anxiety hardly makes for a healthy working environment. Let's hope we've seen the last of that kind of thing here.'

That evening, Lynne phoned her mother to tell her of the day's events. She finished by saying, 'So that certainly takes any pressure off me for making a career move in the near future. I won't rule it out completely, though. The stress and uncertainty that I've been through have got me thinking.'

Audrey was very pleased. 'I'm so glad to hear that things are back on an even keel again. You must give Sarah a ring to let her know. By the way, I haven't heard anything from her son yet. I wonder if she's got any news herself about whether or not he can help me with the house.'

'I'll phone her as soon as we've finished talking,' Lynne promised. 'Mum, it feels so strange being back here, and not being with you and Bob.'

'You're right. But it won't be long before I'm all packed up and moving in with you, and after that, Bob and I will be living in the next street. Lynne, I've been doing some hard thinking.'

'Mum, you don't ever stop these days,' Lynne chided. 'You've got enough on the go now to last you for at least the next six months.'

'I know. But after that I can't just sit in my new home with my feet up! I could get a part time job or do some voluntary work. I could even start a small business.'

'Now that's a thought,' said Lynne. 'A small business… I like the sound of that. Maybe we could do something together.'

'But you've got your job,' her mother replied, surprised. 'And remember, you've got to decide whether or not you're going ahead with looking for a partner. Having me living round the corner mustn't prevent you from putting plenty of thought into that.'

Lynne noticed that she was tempted to change the subject. Instead she confided, 'Mum, I've got to tell you that I nearly ran away from that subject as soon as you mentioned it.'

'I thought you might, and if you had, I would have brought you back to it,' said her mother firmly. 'We've both played a part in avoiding it over the last few years, and we've got to get ourselves out of that habit. I promise I won't push you into anything.'

'Thanks, Mum. Keep up the good work. I'll appreciate it, even if I don't come across as being grateful at times. Shall we ring off now, and I'll phone Sarah. I'll let you know if there's any news about Andy.'

Moments later, Lynne was speaking to Sarah.

'Has Andy phoned your mum yet?' Sarah asked as soon as she heard Lynne's voice.

'Not yet.'

'I think he might be waiting until he's spoken to his electrician friend. But you can tell your mum he's keen to do the plumbing work for her. He got quite excited, and he's hoping she wants to have the bathroom walls tiled. Apparently he's quite a dab hand at that now,' she added proudly. 'Now, tell me how things are at work.'

As Lynne updated her, she made sounds of approval. 'That couldn't be better. To tell you the truth, I hope they postpone appointing anyone, and if Carol holds things together okay, I hope they give her a chance of promotion to the post.'

'I'd like that,' said Lynne. 'I think she'd be a good choice. How are things with you?'

'I've got some wonderful pictures of my little great-niece. I'd like to show them to you some time.'

'How about getting together for an evening here, once Mum's moved across to stay with me? I'm certain she'd like to meet you.'

'I'll look forward to that. Let me know nearer the time, and we'll make a date.'

The next few weeks seemed to flash past. Audrey ordered up a large number of cardboard containers, and sorted through all her possessions, ready for moving. Lynne saw a lot of her at weekends, and they managed to fit in a shopping trip for clothes. Lynne was jubilant when she found a full-length multicoloured skirt in the autumn sales. 'I feel like a mixture of autumn leaves!' she had exclaimed excitedly. 'All these bronze, deep red, orange and yellow hues.' Her mother had insisted on buying it for her, adding that she hoped it was the first of many bright new clothes.

Bob was so much a member of the family that it seemed he had been with them for years rather than weeks. Lynne took him on regular trips to her house, so that he could familiarise himself with it. She blessed the day that they had found him. He was gentle and intelligent, and a good friend and companion. It was almost as if she and her mother could hold a conversation with him.

On the day of the removal, Lynne took a day off work. It was a Friday, which allowed them the weekend together to settle in to their new routine. Lynne put Bob's bed in the conservatory, which was well insulated. The autumn nights were quite mellow, so there was no fear that he would be cold.

Work started on 20 Primrose Terrace on the following Monday. Mr Brown had cleared everything out, and although it was dingy, he had left it clean. First, a neat staircase was installed to give access to the loft. Then replacement windows were fitted throughout. A specialist firm came to install the solar panels, and after that, the new bathroom furniture and kitchen appliances were delivered, ready for Andy to start work. Hardly a day passed without some kind of activity taking place, and Audrey was always on hand to open the door.

She soon became well-acquainted with the family at number eighteen.

'The father's name is Jonas,' she told Lynne. 'Apparently his grandfather was Jamaican. The little boy's name is Louis, and his mum is called Florinda. I met her for the first time yesterday. Sometimes I go and sit in my front garden while I'm waiting to let people in, and if Louis is out playing, he and I have some fascinating conversations. He thinks Bob is wonderful, and of course, Bob's very tolerant.'

Lynne was pleased. 'It's always good to have friendly neighbours. You'll have seen plenty of the people next door to me, and how they keep themselves to themselves, but we help each other out whenever needed.'

'You'll remember Bert Gray across the road from my new home?'

'Yes, that's the man who gave me Tom Brown's phone number at the beginning.'

'He's so pleased that I've taken over the house. He was quite worried about the effect it was having on the neighbourhood. He's been watching everything with an approving eye.'

'That's not a bad sort of person to have around,' Lynne commented. 'He'll not hold back from being critical, but he'll always be fair in his judgements, and he's the kind of person who'll not let anything slip past his eagle gaze.'

'I think that he must work nights. He's certainly got a job of some kind, and whenever I see him, it's always in the afternoon.'

Lynne laughed. 'I think you're just as watchful as he is.'

'As a matter of fact, I've noticed that the curtains in the front bedroom are never closed, so he must sleep in the bedroom at the back.'

Autumn began to fade, and the main work on the house was completed. That left only the interior decoration. Audrey had chosen all the materials and had them at the ready. She had followed through her original idea of employing young offenders, and a small gang of youths arrived, supervised by one of the staff from the halfway houses. They were quite a mixed bunch. There were several who were surprisingly cheerful, and who were clearly very glad of the kudos of this job, but there were two who had little energy, and found it very difficult to get started. Audrey found that she had a strong impulse to start mothering them, but realising that this was not appropriate, she settled instead for doing some home baking, which she delivered to the door each lunchtime.

At the end of the week she was so delighted with the results of their work that she announced that she would pay a bonus. She also told the supervisor that she was willing to write a reference for them on the basis of the quality of the work they had done.

Soon after that, Audrey moved her stored possessions in, Lynne helped her to arrange them, and at last she was ready to sleep her first night in her new home.

'Are you sure you'll be all right?' asked Lynne. 'Oh, this is silly, I'm sounding like a mother hen.'

Audrey looked at her quizzically. 'What do you think's going to happen to me? I'm fit and well. I've got Bob at my side, at least two neighbours who are looking out for me, and you're in the next street. What more could I ever want?'

'Mm... I can see that I'm thinking more about myself,' Lynne admitted. 'I've had the luxury of having you and Bob to come home to for weeks and weeks, and now the house will be empty.'

'Well, over the past months we've been getting my life straightened out, and now it's time to concentrate on yours,' said her mother firmly. 'For a start, remember how we promised ourselves we wouldn't lose sight of your need to think about a partner.'

'Oh dear, I've got that familiar resistance coming up inside me about that particular topic,' Lynne admitted.

'But you've already taken a step forward by being able to say that,' her mother pointed out. 'And the next step is for us to stick to working on our pact of keeping it in our minds. We've no distractions now. My house is finished, and there's nothing else to take priority. Lynne, for a start I think you should join in with some social activities.'

'I see what you mean,' Lynne agreed. 'With the difficulties at work and then your operation and moving house, I'd put all that on one side. I've so enjoyed our time together, and I'd just fallen into that pattern. I'll put my mind to it, and let you know what I come up with.'

'Okay,' her mother approved. 'And my news is that I've decided to look into doing some voluntary work. I phoned the volunteer bureau yesterday, and I'm going along tomorrow to see what's available. Don't worry. I won't take anything on that Bob and I can't really manage. It won't be long before Christmas is here, and I want you and me to be at the ready to make our New Year resolutions after that. Meantime I've been thinking that I'll invite some of the neighbours round for tea and scones some time before Christmas. I've still got some of my homemade jams for people to sample.'

'That's a wonderful idea, Mum!' Lynne exclaimed. 'You can count me in.'

Chapter Twelve

Lynne did not find it easy to turn her mind to her future, but now that her mother was settled and well, she knew that she must. Besides, her mother had made it very clear that she intended to raise the subject regularly. Lynne knew that this could only help, but inside she shied away from dwelling on what these conversations would entail. Each day she tried to make some plans, but quickly found her mind skating off on to other subjects.

The plain truth of the matter was that she did not want to think about anything that might remind her of Larry, and it seemed inevitable that any thoughts about a future partner would bring to mind memories of her time living with him and how it all ended. Try as she might, she could not work out a way round this, and instead kept distracting herself.

However, one thing had definitely changed. Her interest in brightly coloured clothing had not waned, and she often found her mind filling with ideas of what she might search for on her next shopping trip. This was no mere distraction. She felt uplifted by that realisation, and resolved to have a long talk with her mother soon.

An opportunity arose only a couple of days later. Lynne popped into 20 Primrose Terrace on her way home from work, and Audrey suggested that she stay for something to eat. As things worked out, this led to their spending the whole evening together.

They chatted as they prepared some open sandwiches.

'I'm still not sure how to spend my volunteering time,' said Audrey. 'There are so many interesting and worthy options.'

'Take your time in deciding,' Lynne advised.

'I know. Rushing into something certainly would not help.'

'That's all too true,' Lynne agreed in a voice filled with regret.

Audrey glanced at her daughter sharply. She sensed that there was a lot more to be said, but decided to wait. Instead she continued to share her thoughts about volunteering.

'If I'm to be honest, what I'm drawn to the most is doing something with young children. The only problem is that I don't think I've got enough of my energy back yet.'

'Mm... It'll depend on what you're doing. If it's something quite specific, it might be possible.'

'I hadn't thought of that. The image in my mind had been to help out a single parent by taking a child for several hours. But maybe I could offer a particular activity? I'll put my mind to it. I was going to phone the Social Work Department to find out about befriending, but you're right, first I need to work out exactly what I can provide.'

'Mum, I've got something to talk over with you tonight,' Lynne confided decisively.

Audrey smiled. 'Do you want to make a start straight away?'

'No, I'd rather enjoy my food first.'

'Yes, let's. But there's one thing I must remember to ask you.'

'What is it?'

'Have you heard any more about what happened to Lucy?'

'Funny you should ask that. I learned something only today.'

'Tell me.'

'There's a rumour going round that she had been told she was being sent for some retraining.'

'You mean she handed in her notice to avoid that?'

Lynne nodded. 'So the story goes.'

'Well, I sincerely hope that whatever she's involved in now, she mends her ways.'

'So do I,' Lynne agreed with obvious feeling.

After they had finished eating, they made themselves comfortable and Audrey waited for Lynne to begin.

'Mum, I'll have to talk about Larry,' Lynne began abruptly. 'Every time I try to think of a new relationship, I remember what happened, and then I find myself doing some cleaning or tidying.'

'I'm not surprised.' Audrey thought for a few minutes, and then added, 'But maybe it isn't just Larry you need to talk about.'

Lynne was puzzled. It had been obvious to her that it was Larry. What was her mother getting at?

Audrey continued. 'Of course we must talk about Larry, but I think we should be talking about your dad, too.'

'But there was nothing wrong between me and Dad,' Lynne protested. 'And we've been talking a lot about how we both still miss him.'

'That's right. And we must keep on talking about him.'

Lynne hung her head. 'The thing with Larry was horrible,' she said in a low voice. 'I thought he would be the same as Dad. It seemed like that at the beginning, but look how it turned out.'

'We both had our reasons for ignoring the early signs,' Audrey remembered sadly. She reached across and touched her daughter's hand. 'We'll sort this out, and one day you'll find someone who's really right for you.'

'I wish I could believe that,' said Lynne miserably.

'It's a very good sign that you're ready to talk about Larry now,' Audrey pointed out. 'That's a big change.'

'I'm not sure about the "ready",' Lynne stated. 'I don't want to think about him, let alone talk about him, but it seems unavoidable if I want to stop hiding from relationships with men.'

'I think that in time you'll find the talking will mean the remembering doesn't hurt so much,' said Audrey wisely. 'Lynne, you're still quite alone with it all.'

'Mum, you're so right. I've avoided any meaningful contact with all those people who came to the party when I got rid of him, and there were things I never told anyone – not even you.'

'I guessed that, dear. I wonder now if I should have pressed you for more details, but I didn't want you to feel that I was prying.'

'I'm very glad you didn't push me. If you had, I might have started avoiding you.'

'Lynne, I think a door is opening for both of us. Now I've got some strength back, I've been able to insist that you look to your own future, and you've been able to respond. I know it's hard for us both looking back again at your dad's death and your years with Larry, but it's exactly the right thing to do.'

Suddenly all Lynne's reluctance evaporated. 'Okay. Where shall we start?'

'I've got a few photos…'

Before Audrey could finish what she was saying, Lynne shouted, 'I don't want to see them!' Then she fell silent for a moment before adding quietly, 'I burnt all mine before the party.'

Audrey persisted, firmly and gently. 'Come on, we'll do it together.'

Lynne squeezed her eyes tight shut, like a small child.

Determinedly, Audrey laid out four photographs on the coffee table. 'There,' she said.

Lynne opened her eyes slowly and stared at the pictures silently.

Several minutes passed before she spoke. 'I can hardly believe this.'

'Believe what?'

'It's really strange. I thought that if I looked at them, it would somehow seem as if Larry was here now.' Audrey waited, and Lynne continued. 'But actually I know I'm looking at something that happened quite a while ago. It's a piece of history – a nasty piece, but that's what it is.' She turned to her mother. 'I'm so glad you kept these.'

'I must admit I shredded most of them a long time ago, but I had a hunch we might need some one day, so I kept these four.'

'You know something...'

'What is it, dear?'

'If I'd seen photos of him before I met him, I would have been able to see that he was a crook. It was all that sweet talk and patter that took me in. He was a genius at that.' Lynne giggled. 'Maybe I should make a hobby of looking at photos of men, and grading them in order of suitability. And if Dad was here, I'm sure he'd take a keen interest.'

'Sadly, I think that if your dad had still been alive then, he would have seen through Larry right from the beginning.'

Lynne's face became serious. 'I've no doubt at all that you're right.'

They sat quietly for a while, each lost in their own thoughts.

Then suddenly Lynne announced, 'The badminton club! Mum, I've got to face the badminton club. That's definitely the next step. I'll go round tomorrow and see what I have to do to fix up my membership again.'

Audrey gazed at her daughter. It was as if a transformation was taking place.

Chapter Thirteen

The next day, Lynne went round to the badminton club straight after work. She noted with pleasure that everything had been repainted since she was last there. This meant that although the building had not changed, it looked different. How silly to have avoided coming here for so long, she thought. She had avoided the whole street for years, thinking that this would protect her from some of the pain. What nonsense! She was glad that she could see through her defensive behaviour now. It had done her no good at all.

She did not recognise the slender young woman at the desk.

'I was once a member here,' Lynne explained. 'Can I sign up again?'

'Certainly.' The woman searched for some forms and handed them to Lynne saying, 'If your membership lapsed less than five years ago, we'll still have your details on the system, so you won't need to provide references.'

'It was definitely less than five years ago,' Lynne replied firmly. She took the forms to a quiet corner.

She was soon back at the desk, handing over the forms and paying the fee. The young woman quickly made up a membership card for her.

'Do you play here yourself?' Lynne asked casually.

The woman nodded.

Lynne hesitated only for a second. 'Fancy a game sometime?'

The woman's face broke into a smile. 'Yes, of course. I'm Mandy.'

'I'm a bit rusty,' Lynne warned cheerfully.

'I'm not a serious player,' Mandy told her. 'I come for the social life. There's a good bunch of people here, and we have plenty of fun.'

'Great! You can count me in.'

'Let's sign up now for our game,' Mandy suggested. She led the way to the boards where the booking sheets were displayed. 'How about tomorrow?'

'Suits me. I've come straight from work, so this time would be ideal.'

'It's just before the rush starts.' Mandy grinned at Lynne. 'I'll give you the names of the people to avoid. There aren't many of them I'm glad to say. They're devils on the courts, and they aren't the sort of people you'd want as friends, either.'

'Thanks. That's really helpful.' Lynne did not say more. Mandy would probably never know just how helpful she was being.

As she was leaving, Lynne called over her shoulder, 'I'll look forward to tomorrow.'

'Me, too,' Mandy replied.

Lynne went straight home, but phoned her mother as soon as she got in.

'I've got some good news, and I'll pop round later to tell you.'

'Sounds interesting. I'll keep guessing until you arrive.'

'See you around nine.'

After finishing the call, Lynne went straight to the storage cupboard under the stairs. She had to bend nearly double as she rummaged around in its dusky depths.

'Ah! Here it is!' she exclaimed triumphantly as her hand made contact with a flattish cardboard box. She pulled it out into the light, and then took it into the sitting room. After that, she took several deep breaths to steady herself, before easing off the lid to reveal the glorious dress she had worn at the 'getting rid of Larry' party. She gasped. It really was beautiful. It was the only thing she had saved from those terrible times, and she had not looked at it since she packed it away after the party was over.

As if mesmerised by the dress, she took off her office clothes and stepped into it. It fitted her as if the party had been only yesterday. The elegantly-cut sleeveless style showed off her figure perfectly.

Aloud she said determinedly, 'This is too good a dress not to be worn again. I must find a suitable occasion.' She stroked the material over her abdomen. Suddenly she shuddered. Thank goodness she had never got pregnant. He had often pressed her, but she had been certain that she should wait a little longer. Thank goodness he had not forced her. Instinct told her now that the day would have come, had she not first exposed him.

Eventually she replaced the dress in the box, although she did not return it to its place in the cupboard. Instead, she decided to keep it readily accessible, in her bedroom. This accomplished, she put on some casual clothes, and then glanced at her watch.

Goodness! she thought. It was already nearly nine. Where had all that time gone? Yet in her heart she knew very well that she had been on a particular journey – one where today's time had been of no consequence. Feeling no pangs of hunger, she decided to make something later, and she hurried round to her mother's house.

'I did it!' she announced as soon as she arrived.

'Did what?' her mother enquired.

'You know… the badminton club. It all went fine, and I've booked a game for tomorrow with Mandy – the person who helped me renew my membership. I think she's a bit younger than I am, but she's just my kind of person, and from what she told me, there are plenty of pleasant people amongst the members.'

'That's wonderful news. Did you…'

'If you're going to ask if I felt wobbly while I was there, I'm glad to report that I didn't. I think it helped that the place had been repainted, but the main thing is that I was determined to get back what I had enjoyed.'

72

'You've certainly made a good start. Is there any more news?'

Lynne shook her head. Audrey detected a hint of something she couldn't quite put her finger on, but said nothing. Then Lynne's stomach rumbled loudly.

'Mum, I'm starving.'

'Help yourself to anything in the kitchen. There's a nice piece of quiche in the fridge.' Audrey smiled inwardly. For a moment, Lynne had sounded like an eager adolescent, and she sensed it was a good sign.

Chapter Fourteen

From then on, Lynne managed to fit in a game of badminton most evenings, and she soon got to know plenty of the people at the club. She began to feel quite fit, and her mother commented on how well she looked. Mandy had been right in saying that the social life was good. The club members fixed up at least one event every month, and Lynne took part. They were always such fun. There was a good mix of people – with a range of ages and situations.

In the end, Audrey had decided to give herself more time before she took on any volunteering responsibilities. She let herself enjoy a quiet easy life, pottering around with Bob.

Every night, before she went to bed, Lynne would open the flat cardboard box and gaze at the dress. Sometimes she would take it out and lay it on the bed. Sometimes she would put it on for a while.

Some months later, several new people joined the group at the club, and Lynne quickly got to know them all. She discovered that one of them, Joy, lived at the other end of Primrose Terrace, and had noticed the changes at number 20. Joy was the same age as Lynne, and she was trying to get fit again now that her three children were all school age. They quickly became friends, and Lynne introduced Joy to her mother and Bob.

Not long afterwards, Lynne learned that Joy had a brother who was moving to the area to start a new job.

'His wife died,' explained Joy matter-of-factly, although Lynne noticed that she looked quite upset. 'He wanted a complete change, and I suggested he moved near me so he could see more of us. I was very relieved when he decided to go ahead and follow my advice.'

Lynne wanted to ask if he had any children, but she didn't think it was the right moment. Instead she said, 'I'm very sorry to hear about his wife. Was she ill for long?'

'She was in a road accident nearly a year ago. At first the doctors thought she would survive, but she died of the injuries a few weeks later.' Joy took out a tissue and wiped tears from her eyes. Then she continued. 'She was a lovely person. It's a terrible loss.'

Lynne put a hand on her friend's arm. 'I'm so sorry to hear all this, but I'm very glad you told me. What's your brother's name?'

'Stuart.'

For a fraction of a second, Lynne felt sick. That was Larry's middle name. Determinedly, she thrust the thought to one side. She could think about it later, in the privacy of her home. After all, the name was a good one. It was the association that was bad.

'I like that name,' she said warmly.

'He was called after our grandad – Mum's father. He was a wonderful man.'

'When does he start his new job?'

'In a few weeks' time. I think it's around the end of May. He'll be staying with us at first.' She laughed. 'It'll be a bit of a squeeze, but I'm so looking forward to having him. The children are really excited too. He's had his house on the market, and he's just heard he's got a buyer. I think he's planning to put his furniture in store and then start to house-hunt in earnest once he's here.'

Lynne made a mental note to talk to her mother about this situation. Maybe she would consider the possibility of Stuart sleeping at her house.

It was the following week by the time Lynne had a chance to tell her mother what she had learned.

'Poor man,' said Audrey in heartfelt tones. 'Nothing will ease that pain for some time yet.' She fell silent, and Lynne observed that she had drawn into herself. She said nothing more, and waited quietly. Then Audrey leaned forward in her chair and said seriously, 'You must tell Joy that she can bring him round to meet me... In fact, you could let her know that I could offer him a bed while he's looking for a new home, if that would help.'

'I thought you would say that. I didn't say anything to Joy, because I didn't want you to feel under any pressure, but I'll let her know tomorrow, when I see her at the club.'

'I think I might take a walk down to see her before then,' Audrey decided. 'I'd rather speak to her myself.'

'That sounds even better,' Lynne agreed.

Chapter Fifteen

Everything had fallen into place quite neatly. Audrey's conversation with Joy had led to an arrangement that Stuart would sleep at her house, but would spend most of his free time with Joy's family.

He arrived on the Saturday evening before the first week in his new post. Lynne was waiting with her mother to greet him. When the doorbell rang, she jumped to her feet to let him in. Bob sat up immediately and followed her into the hall.

Her first impression of Stuart was of someone who looked quite boyish, although at the same time careworn. She guessed he must be a few inches taller than herself, and he was of medium build. His hair was very short. His features certainly reminded her a little of Joy. He was carrying a large backpack, and was dressed in casual clothes.

She greeted him. 'Hello, you must be Stuart. I'm Lynne.'

Bob reached forward and licked his hand. Stuart patted his head saying, 'Good dog. Pleased to meet you.'

'Come on in,' Lynne invited. She opened the door wide and pointed towards the sitting room. 'Audrey, my mum, is looking forward to meeting you.'

'Thanks. It's very kind of her to help. I can't say how much I appreciate it.'

Lynne noticed how straight away she liked the sound of his voice. There was something about it that produced a very pleasant feeling in her.

'Mum, it's Stuart,' she called.

Audrey appeared at the door of the sitting room and held out her hand. 'It's good to meet you, Stuart. Come and sit down. I hope your journey was comfortable.'

'Fine, thanks.'

'I'll put the kettle on,' Lynne offered. 'We've got a good selection of teas. Have you any preferences?'

'Anything's fine for me,' Stuart replied.

Bob lay down close to him, resting his head on his feet.

'I hope you'll be comfortable in the attic,' Audrey began. 'There's plenty of space, and we've put a good-quality futon up there.'

'Sounds more than I deserve.'

Audrey did not challenge this slightly curious response. Instead she said, 'I'll leave it up to you to ask if there's anything else you need. I've put breakfast cereals in the kitchen, and you can help yourself whenever you want.'

He smiled. 'Thanks. Looks as if I can have two breakfasts a day – one here, and one at Joy's.'

Lynne appeared with the tea and passed round the mugs.

Stuart looked at Audrey and cleared his throat. 'Before I put my things upstairs, I must finalise the arrangements with you.'

Audrey looked puzzled. 'Have I forgotten something?'

'I should pay something in advance, and then whatever weekly charge you make.'

'Oh goodness!' Audrey exclaimed. 'You're a guest here, not a lodger.' She added unguardedly, 'You've had a pretty hard time of late, and what you need is some kindness.'

Lynne saw Stuart's face twitch, and he quickly reached down to fondle Bob's ears.

'Er… But I understand you told Joy I could stay here as long as I needed.'

'That's correct,' Audrey assured him.

'Well, I couldn't possibly do that without at least contributing to the costs.'

Here Lynne intervened. 'Could you agree to be a guest for a month?' she suggested. 'After that, we could review the whole situation.'

Audrey nodded. 'How about that, Stuart?'

Stuart's face relaxed. 'That's a wonderful offer. And

Audrey, if there are any odd jobs you'd like me to do, don't ever hesitate to ask. I'm quite handy with tools.'

'That's good to know,' Audrey replied. 'I'll see if anything comes up.'

Stuart persisted. 'Don't wait for that. You might like to think up a little project.'

Audrey considered this. 'That's a very interesting offer. I'll bear it in mind.'

Audrey noticed that she fell into the new routine without any difficulty. After only a week or so, it felt as if Stuart had been with them for a lot longer, and was already an established part of their lives. She had begun to toy with the idea of asking him if he might be able to build a shed for her in the back garden, but had not mentioned anything yet.

On reflection, Lynne began to realise that Joy, Stuart and Joy's husband, Ian, were to her as siblings were to people from larger families. The only thing that was out of place was that Stuart never referred to his wife, Esme. Lynne had learned her name from Joy, but Stuart had never spoken it.

Joy had invited Stuart to join the badminton club, but he had declined, stating firmly that he'd far rather stay with Ian and play with the children while she went out. Lynne learned that bedtimes without Joy were already becoming a longed-for experience by the children, who encouraged their mother to play as many games of badminton as she wanted. Apparently Uncle Stuart was a wonderful reader of bedtime stories. Not only did he read the stories, but also he often acted some of the characters.

After a month at Audrey's house, Stuart insisted on paying her a weekly sum that would more than cover the extra expenses of his living there. Audrey tried to brush this plan to one side, but he would not give in.

'And we must have a review in a few weeks' time,' he added firmly. 'I've been keeping a close eye on the housing market, but nothing much is shifting around here at the moment that's in my price bracket.'

'If you're still here in a month's time, I've a possible project to discuss with you,' Audrey told him.

Stuart pressed her, but she would not tell him what she had in mind. 'Maybe by then you'll have found a house to do up, and you won't have time for unnecessary frivolities.'

Stuart raised his eyebrows, but said no more.

Meanwhile, Joy's children had made it very clear that they wanted Mummy and Daddy to go away for a night in the summer holidays, and leave them in the care of Uncle Stuart and Auntie Lynne. Lynne and Stuart fell in with this plan readily, and encouraged Joy and Ian to think of a whole weekend away rather than only one night.

'I can stay at Mum's for those nights,' Lynne suggested. 'I'll go there once they're all settled in bed, and you can phone me any time of the night for reinforcements if needed. It'll only take me a minute to run down the road.'

Chapter Sixteen

By the time the weekend away was near, Stuart had nearly completed a brand new shed in Audrey's garden. She was delighted with it, particularly as they had chosen one that would allow her to sit in it with the door open and enjoy the fresh air.

Joy and Ian had chosen a destination that reminded them of their early days together, and the children were full of barely-suppressed excitement. After tea on the Friday evening they waved their parents goodbye and rushed back into the house to issue a stream of instructions to Lynne and Stuart, who found it difficult to remain straight-faced.

Bedtime was a glorious experience of water fights followed by makeshift theatre, and the last pair of eyes did not finally shut until well after ten o'clock.

'Phew!' said Stuart as he and Lynne tiptoed into the kitchen for a cup of tea.

Stuart filled the kettle with water and switched it on. While he was still turned away from her, Lynne heard him say, 'Being with them is the only thing that makes life bearable since Esme's death.' Then he turned towards her and said brightly, 'What kind of brew are you after?'

As they sat drinking their tea together, Lynne decided to say something. 'I heard what you said about Esme,' she began, 'and I can entirely understand it. I haven't suffered that kind of loss, but the person who was to be my life's partner turned out to be a dangerous conman. I was lucky to be able to finish it without any injury.'

They stared at each other across the kitchen table. 'When was that?' asked Stuart.

'Three years ago.'

'Mine's terribly raw.'

'Although I've had longer than you, in some ways mine is too. I met him at the badminton club, and I've only recently been able to rejoin.'

Stuart took this in, but said nothing.

By this time, Lynne's tea was finished. She stood up and announced, 'That's me off. See you in the morning, around eight, but remember, you only have to lift the phone any time and I'll be with you in a trice.'

He chuckled, and she left, pausing only fleetingly to wave to him before she pulled the front door shut behind her.

When she reached number 20, her mother was in bed and was likely to be asleep. She had a quick wash, and then climbed the narrow stairs to the attic, where she put on a thin summer nightie, left her mobile phone handy and snuggled down on the futon. The futon seemed to have a faint pleasant smell about it. Sleepily she thought it must be the new wood in the framework, but then it came to her that the smell reminded her of Stuart.

She slept very soundly. Her dreams were full of memories of her father and of Larry, together with images of closeness with Stuart that she had never consciously entertained.

The harsh buzzing of the alarm on her mobile phone jolted Lynne awake. Hastily, she made herself ready and returned to number 20 to be ready to make breakfasts.

Inside Joy's house, everything was completely silent. Fear gripped her. What had happened? Then she peeped into the main bedroom and saw in the dim light that there were four people in the double bed – one large and three small. She put a hand over her mouth to muffle her giggles, backed into the hall, and retreated to the kitchen. She took a recipe book out of a cupboard, and studied it quietly. It was very interesting, as it contained traditional recipes from around the world.

It was well after ten before Stuart emerged. He staggered into the kitchen, mumbling 'What time is it?'

Lynne looked up from her book and could not help laughing at the bleary-eyed worn-out form that was leaning against the worktop. He was dressed only in thin pyjama bottoms.

'Sit down and I'll put the kettle on,' Lynne instructed kindly.

Stuart slid onto one of the kitchen chairs, putting his arms on the table, and laying his head on them, eyes shut.

'I'm completely worn out,' he moaned.

'That's pretty obvious. What happened?'

'The patter of little feet started soon after midnight, and soon I had them all in bed with me, demanding stories. I must have fallen asleep in the middle of it all, and for the rest of the night I drifted in and out of consciousness as they piled themselves on me as if I were an extra-large teddy bear.'

'In that case I think we should stay in here and let them sleep on.'

Stuart sat bolt upright, and nearly toppled off his chair. 'But if we do that, they'll be awake until goodness knows when tonight.'

'In that case we'll give them another hour, and then spend the afternoon at the swimming pool to wear them out.'

Stuart stared at her in admiration. 'How would I manage without you?'

'Don't be silly. You'd be fine.'

'Fine, but in a bit of a muddle I should think.'

Lynne conceded this and offered to make him some breakfast.

Stuart stood up. 'That's a kind offer, but I'd better get a shower and put some clean clothes on.'

'You might wake them up,' Lynne warned.

He slumped back into the chair. 'How right you are. I'll wait here for a while.'

Silently Lynne handed him a mug of tea and a bowl of muesli.

'Esme and I were about to start a family,' said Stuart, staring hard at the mug.

'I thought that Larry and I would have children. I'm so glad we didn't. It would have been dreadful.'

'The children or the father?' Stuart's eyes were still fixed firmly on the mug.

'The father of course.'

'I can't plan anything at the moment. Might you…'

Just then the three children crept into the kitchen and leapt on him from behind.

'Yeow!' he shrieked.

Lynne took charge. 'Your Uncle Stuart needs to have his breakfast in peace.'

'Why?' chorused three voices.

'Otherwise he won't have the energy to come with us to the swimming pool.'

The three small people jumped up and down excitedly. 'Swimming pool! Swimming pool! Hooray!'

'Come and sit round the table, and I'll make something nice for you,' Lynne promised. 'I've been reading this recipe book. Perhaps I can make a breakfast from another country.'

The rest of the day passed without any undue stress. Although the swimming pool was busy, most of the people there were families with young children, and the atmosphere was very pleasant. As Lynne had predicted, their three gradually exhausted themselves while she and Stuart kept an eye on them.

The evening was quite different from the previous one. The children ate early, and then begged to go to bed, saying that they would have some stories in the morning. By eight, there was no sound from their rooms.

Stuart flopped down on the sofa in the sitting room. 'I'm completely clapped out,' he announced.

'It looks as if you'd better go to bed yourself,' Lynne observed with a smile. 'I'll go and spend the rest of the evening with Mum.'

Stuart looked disappointed, but said nothing. Lynne gathered her things and prepared to leave.

'Remember to phone if you need me.'

'Lynne… Would you like to stay for an hour or so?'

Stuart's voice was uncertain and jerky.

'Of course. Mum's not expecting me until later.' Lynne put her things on a low table, and sat down. 'We should make some plans for tomorrow,' she said brightly.

'If it's dry, we could go to the adventure playground. It's only a short bus journey away. If it's wet, we could stay here and play games or do puzzles and things like that, and perhaps throw in a visit to the museum. There's quite a lot there that would interest them.'

'You seem to have it all worked out.'

Stuart nodded. 'Self-preservation – in its best possible sense.' He paused and then said, 'As you know, I'm looking for a house, but I don't know what kind of house I want.'

'It can be tricky, I know,' Lynne sympathised. 'I was lucky with mine. It's always seemed just right for one.'

'The problem is that I don't know exactly what I'll be using it for.'

Lynne looked at him, perplexed. 'What would you want it for as well as for living in?'

Stuart opened his mouth, but nothing came out, so he shut it again. He stared at her for a minute.

'Er... Tomorrow is my wedding anniversary.'

Lynne's hand flew to her mouth. 'Oh! I'm so sorry. I wish you'd said something before.'

'I thought I didn't need to, but now I realise I did.' Stuart's eyes filled with tears.

Lynne grabbed a box of tissues from a shelf and thrust it at him.

'Thanks,' he muttered.

'Stuart, if you want to talk about it sometime, Mum and I could sit with you one evening. I don't need to ask her, because she's that sort of person. Let us know.' She stood up. 'I'm glad you told me. See you in the morning... that is...' she smiled '... unless you radio for help before then.'

Stuart smiled back at her, and for a moment a warmth flowed between them. Then she turned, and was gone.

85

Audrey was listening to some music, but she switched it off when she heard Lynne come in.

'It's nice to see you, dear. How did it go?'

Lynne recounted the day's events with the children, and Audrey laughed heartily at some of her descriptions.

'The pair of you seem to be making a good job of things,' she commented when Lynne had finished.

'I'm certain we'll survive. Joy and Ian are due back around midnight on Sunday, so we'll try our best to wear the kids out tomorrow for them. Stuart's got some plans.'

'He's doing so well,' Audrey commented, 'despite the fact that he must still be in a state of shock.'

'He tried to talk a bit this evening. I thought it was the wrong time, so I suggested he could talk to us both here one evening.'

'That was very wise of you, dear.'

'Mum…'

'What is it?'

'To be honest, I thought that if he and I talked this evening, we might have ended up in a clinch, and for all the wrong reasons.'

'You did absolutely the right thing,' Audrey approved. 'One day this week I'll sound him out gently about whether or not he'd like a chat – with me, or with both of us.'

Sunday passed very pleasantly. The day was warm and dry, and Lynne made up a substantial picnic to take to the adventure playground. Stuart loaded it into his backpack, and they set off for the bus.

They did not return home until nearly six o'clock. By that time the children were ready for more food, a bath, and then storytime. Again, eight o'clock saw them fast asleep.

'That's me off then,' Lynne announced as she collected her things together. 'I'll go back home now and get my things ready for work tomorrow.'

'The others shouldn't be long before they're back,' said

Stuart, half to himself. Then suddenly he surprised her by saying, 'Lynne, thanks for a wonderful weekend. I'll never forget it.'

Lynne knew that he was being sincere. She smiled across at him. 'Thank you, too.'

He did not move towards her, but the way his eyes held Lynne's gaze felt to her as if he had given her a hug.

'Bye then,' she said lightly, and was soon heading towards her home.

Chapter Seventeen

Monday at work for Lynne was unremarkable, although it was punctuated regularly by remembered scenes from the weekend that brought a smile to her face. As the day passed, she realised she had much to talk over with her mother, and so she decided to call in to see her on the way home.

As she neared number 20, she found Bob snoozing on the front doorstep. He became immediately alert at the sound of her approaching. His single quiet 'woof' brought Audrey to the door.

She greeted Lynne. 'Hello, dear, I was hoping you might call by.'

'I could do with having a chat about the weekend,' Lynne explained.

'I'm not surprised. And I can tell you there's quite a change in Stuart.'

Soon they were sitting together, deep in conversation.

'Being with the children like that has left me feeling very clear that I would definitely like to have children of my own,' Lynne confided.

'I wondered if that might happen.'

'I know it's no good rushing into things, but I do feel really at ease with Stuart.'

'He certainly feels the same about you. We had a long conversation when he got back last night. I was glad I was still up. He came in just after ten, saying that Joy and Ian had come back a bit earlier than expected. We sat up until after midnight. It was as if a stopper had come out. He talked and talked. Everything he had been holding back since Esme's accident came pouring out. Before he went to bed, he asked if I thought you might be interested in him.'

'What did you say?'

'I said I knew you liked him a lot.'

Lynne struggled with a strong impulse to grill her mother about everything, but instead she asked calmly, 'Did he say anything after that?'

'He said he knew that it was all too soon, and he asked if I thought you would wait for him. I told him to ask you about that.'

Back home, Lynne went straight to her bedroom, and took out the dress.

'I was right to keep it,' she murmured as she stroked the skirt, 'but I don't need to wear it again. And once things are clearer between me and Stuart, I'll give it away to a good home.'

The next time she saw Stuart, he was sitting in the tiny front garden of Joy's house, relaxing. As soon as he saw her, he jumped to his feet and went to meet her.

'I've been missing you,' he said awkwardly.

'You're never far from my thoughts,' Lynne told him.

Stuart cleared his throat nervously. 'As you know, I've got a lot to sort out. I don't know how long it will all take.' He stopped, and Lynne could see he looked quite worried. He seemed to want to say something else, but couldn't get started, so she waited quietly. 'Er... Will you wait for me?'

'So long as we can do some more outings with the children meantime,' said Lynne with a smile.

He beamed at her and gave her a quick hug. 'That won't be difficult. They've been plotting to send Joy and Ian away again soon.'

Emily by Mirabelle Maslin

ISBN 978-0-9549551-8-2   £8.99

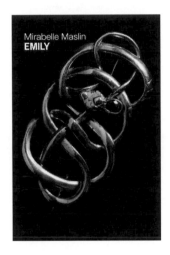

Orphaned by the age of ten, Emily lives with her Aunt Jane. While preparing to move house, they come across an old diary of Jane's, and she shows Emily some intriguing spiral patterns that appeared in it just before she, Emily, was born. Clearly no passing curiosity, these patterns begin to affect Emily in ways that no one can understand, and as time passes, something momentous begins to form in their lives. While studying at university, Emily meets Barnaby. Sensing that they have been drawn together for a common purpose, they discover that each carries a crucial part of an unfinished puzzle from years past. It is only then that Emily's true purpose is revealed.

Events in 'Emily' are foreshadowed in Mirabelle Maslin's 'Beyond the Veil' and 'Fay'.

Order from your local bookshop, amazon.co.uk or the augurpress website at www.augurpress.com

Beyond the Veil by Mirabelle Maslin
ISBN 0-9549551-4-5   £8.99

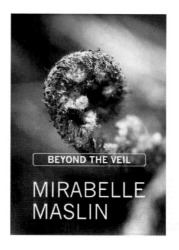

Spiral patterns, a strange tape of music from Russia, a 'blank' book and an oddly-carved walking stick…

Ellen encounters Adam, a young widower, and a chain of mysterious and unpredictable events begins to weave their lives together.   Chance, contingency and coincidence all play a part – involving them with friends in profound experiences, and lifting the pall of loss that has been affecting both their lives.

Against a backdrop of music, plant lore, mysterious writing and archaeology, the author touches on deeper issues of bereavement, friendship, illness and the impact of objects from the past on our lives. Altered states, heightened sensitivities and unseen communications are explored, as is the importance of caring and mutual understanding.

The story culminates in an experience of spiritual ecstasy, leading separate paths to an unusual and satisfying convergence.

**Order from your local bookshop, amazon, or from the Augur Press
website www.augurpress.com**

Fay by Mirabelle Maslin
ISBN 0-9549551-3-7   £8.99

Fay is suffering from a mysterious illness.   Her family and friends are concerned about her. In her vulnerable state, she begins to be affected by something more than intuition, and at first no one can make sense of it.

Alongside the preparation for her daughter's wedding, she is drawn into new situations together with resonances of lives that are long past, and at last the central meaning of her struggles begins to emerge.

Order from your local bookshop, amazon, or from the Augur Press website www.augurpress.com

The Fifth Key by Mirabelle Maslin

ISBN 978–0–9558936–0–5   £7.99

Soon after Nicholas' thirteenth birthday, his great-uncle John reveals to him a secret – handed down through hundreds of years to the 'chosen one' in every second generation. John is very old. His house has long since fallen into disrepair, and as Nicholas begins to learn about the fifth key and the pledge, John falls ill. Facing these new challenges and helping to repair John's house, Nicholas begins to discover his maturing strengths.

The unexpected appearance of Jake, the traveller whom Nicholas has barely known as his much older brother, heralds a sequence of events that could never have been predicted, and a bond grows between the brothers that evolves beyond the struggles of their ancestors and of Jake's early life.

Order from your local bookshop, amazon.co.uk or the augurpress website at www.augurpress.com

he Candle Flame by Mirabelle Maslin

ISBN 978-0-9558936-1-2   £7.99

One dark winter's night, an unseen force attacks Molly, leaving her for dead. On their return from snaring rabbits, her husband, Sam, and his brothers, James and Alec, discover her, and slowly nurse her back to life. But she cannot speak. Determined to avenge Molly and help her to regain her voice, the brothers search for clues. Could her affliction be due to a curse? The birth of Sam and Molly's son, Nathan, raises questions about his ancestry. Who was Molly's father, and how did he meet his end? Might there be a connection between violent events of long ago and Molly's present state?

Order from your local bookshop, amazon.co.uk or the augurpress website at www.augurpress.com

Also available from Augur Press

The Poetry Catchers by Pupils from Craigton Primary School	£7.99	978-0-9549551-9-9
Beyond the Veil by Mirabelle Maslin	£8.99	0-9549551-4-5
Fay by Mirabelle Maslin	£8.99	0-9549551-3-7
Emily by Mirabelle Maslin	£8.99	978-0-9549551-8-2
Miranda by Mirabelle Maslin	£6.99	978-0-9558936-5-0
Hemiplegic Utopia: Manc Style by Lee Seymour	£6.99	978-0-9549551-7-5
Carl and other writings by Mirabelle Maslin	£5.99	0-9549551-2-9
Letters to my Paper Lover by Fleur Soignon	£7.99	0-9549551-1-0
On a Dog Lead by Mirabelle Maslin	£6.99	978-0-9549551-5-1
Poems of Wartime Years by W N Taylor	£4.99	978-0-9549551-6-8
The Fifth Key by Mirabelle Maslin	£7.99	978-0-9558936-0-5
The Candle Flame by Mirabelle Maslin	£7.99	978-0-9558936-1-2
Mercury in Dental Fillings by Stewart J Wright	£5.99	978-0-9558936-2-9
The Voice Within by Catherine Turvey	£5.99	978-0-9558936-3-6
The Supply Teacher's Surprise by Mirabelle Maslin	£5.99	978-0-9558936-4-3
Tracy by Mirabelle Maslin	£6.95	0-9549551-0-2

Ordering:	Postage and packing – £1.00 per title
By post	Delf House, 52, Penicuik Road, Roslin, Midlothian EH25 9LH UK
By e-mail	info@augurpress.com
Online	www.augurpress.com (credit cards accepted)

Cheques payable to Augur Press. Prices and availability subject to change without notice. When placing your order, please mention if you do not wish to receive any additional information.

www.augurpress.com

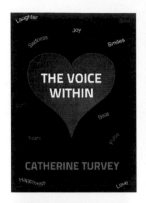

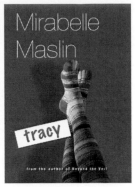

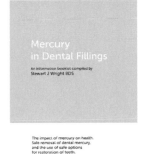

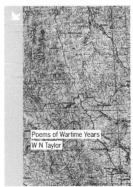

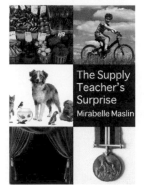

'Miranda' is another title in the self-help series.